What Life
Was Like
When I Was
a Kid

Also by the author:

The Brandon Family of Southwest Florida

The Descendants of James and Mary Cupples Hanna

What Life Was Like When I Was a Kid

by James S. Hanna, Sr.

The Naylor Company
Book Publishers of the Southwest
San Antonio, Texas

Library of Congress Cataloging in Publication Data

Hanna, James Scott, 1897-1972.
    What life was like when I was a kid.

    1. Hanna, James Scott, 1897-1972.
I. Title.
CT275.H3615A33   1973   917.64'139'0360924 [B]   73-19538
ISBN 0-8111-0510-5

To my wife, my four children, and my grandchildren.

*A Tribute Given at the Funeral Service of
James Scott Hanna, Sr. Written By His
Grandson, Scott Ingersoll Harmon*

*James Scott Hanna was truly a renaissance man. Like
a Leonardo da Vinci or a Thomas Jefferson, he found
in life a constant enjoyment; not only in living, but also
in every aspect of the universe that confronted him. He
strove continually for excellence in all that he did. There
was never enough time for him to discover all that he
wanted to know about the sciences, music, philosophy
or the infinite variations of man and his achievements.
He was not only a scholar; he loved to work with his
hands whether it was sculpture or painting or wood-
work. His strength of character, leadership, and diversity
of interest made him a success in business as well as in
all other endeavors to which he turned his hand.*

*Like those intellects of the renaissance, he found in each
day a myriad of interests and a sense of awakening and
rebirth in his own mind.*

*His love of his family and his intense appreciation of life
and all it had to offer will be with us as his best legacy.
He would not want us to grieve, but to remember him
and cherish his legacy as the valuable thing it is.*

Contents

Introduction

Why This Book Was Written

While I was workng on the genealogy and history of our branch of the Hanna family early in 1963 and, later, on the Brandon genealogy, I found very little recorded on the individual and personal activities of even the most recent ancestors. Childhood activities, such as popular games, pranks or social edicts violated, were blank. In checking further, I found this condition characteristic of any given era of boys' lifc in the past. This is, indeed, most unfortunate, for the earliest years of life are often the most interesting, and even though only a tiny facet of history may be represented by the era, it would be difficult indeed to find any two groups whose culture, behavior, and physical activities were very similar.

As a closing paragraph to this introduction, let me

assure the reader that all events related herein are strictly factual. Surnames of prominent older citizens have been used only where necessary to support historical background. For the childhood companions who participated in the activities I have recorded here, only the first names or nicknames are used. Those who are still living will recognize their names and the part they played in this drama.

J. S. H.
Lake Travis,
Leander, Texas

Chapter 1

My First Memories

In order that the reader may be properly oriented as to time, let me first state that I was born on August 30, 1897, in my parents' home in Galveston, Texas.

It would still be some months before the battleship *Maine* was to be blown up in Havana Harbor and the Spanish-American War would begin. The steam railroads were continuing their expansion in all parts of the country, and the automobile, as a popular and universal means of transportation, was not to come for another ten years.

People of even moderate means maintained a horse and buggy, while the well-to-do drove a team of sleek bays hitched to a carriage, a surrey or a victoria. For travelling beyond the city there was the railroad, while, for those whose destination was New York, the weekly sailings of the passenger steamers of the Mallory Line were well patronized.

With the development of the electric generator nearly all cities soon had electric power available for lighting streets and homes, and for the operation of streetcars on which one could ride for many miles for the price of only five cents. Galveston was no exception, and also boasted an artificial gas generating plant which had replaced the oil lamp at least twenty years before. Relatively few homes could afford the cost of gas for cooking, and for a number of years to come use of the iron range with wood or coal for fuel was the general practice. The telephone, such as it was, with magneto ringing and wet cell battery for talking current, had been in use for about ten years; but a heavy rain or stiff breeze usually put the system out of service for several days.

This, then, was the average picture of modern living in most American cities at the time I was born and was typical of the town where I was to spend my childhood. Though many changes in this pattern of life were to take place, they came about gradually. Some of these were momentous events in my life which I remember vividly, such as the time when father had our big home wired for electricity, which thereby made the long wax taper for lighting our gas chandeliers a thing of the past. This, however, did not happen until I was ten years old; so it is as clear in my memory as though it occurred a week ago.

There was another event which I remember very well because it made a big change in our mode of living. This was the installation of copper screens in all windows and doors. A factory representative was sent down from the North to make the installation. When the job was finished,

2

all the mosquito bars were removed from our beds, never to be used again.

Some of the early events in my life are not so easy to remember, and there are always these questions: Do I actually remember that event as it occurred? Or do I remember it as described by others? According to some psychologists, there can be no memory of events which transpired prior to the time we learned to talk and were able to put into words the things we saw and heard. Be that as it may, I find it impossible to recall any events in my life until I was past three years of age, although, according to my mother, I was talking before my third birthday. For example, on August 30, 1900, I was three years old. Eight days later Galveston was struck by the great hurricane which took eight thousand lives, and there is not a single incident in those hours of horror that I can recall. Perhaps my vocabulary had not reached that degree of verbalization needed to recall such unusual events onto the magnetic tape of my memory system, or perhaps I was just too frightened. But, in the days and months which followed I can recall many of the details of the storm as related by my father to visitors in our home and to relatives whom we visited later.

That fateful day started out just like any other, although the sky was overcast and strong winds blew steadily from the northeast. There was no warning of an approaching hurricane such as we receive today many days in advance. In the absence of such a warning system we never knew how severe this storm was to be or where it would strike the coast, until it had come and gone. Businessmen went to their offices as usual that morning, taking the extra precaution of lugging an umbrella or a raincoat. Before noon it had started to rain, and when Father came home for lunch he reported rather gravely that water in the bay had backed up and was now over the level of the wharves and coming up into the business district. The wind, too, had increased in intensity and by midafternoon our big two-story house trembled slightly as the heavier gusts struck. Father did not return to the office, and a neighbor dropped by to report that houses along the beach on the gulf side of the island had begun to break up from the wave action of the high tides. By five o'clock the water was four feet deep in our yard and Father decided to abandon our house and seek greater safety in a large brick house of one of our neighbors across the alley about two hundred feet away. Just to make this decision must have required quite a bit of courage, for Mother was then three months pregnant with her fifth child, besides whom there were four young children and two Negro servants. I do not know how many trips my father made shepherding us all over to our neighbors' home, but I do remember being told that my Negro mammy, Anice, carried me in her arms wading through water up to her breasts.

During the night the big hurricane reached its maximum intensity with winds which registered over one hundred miles per hour, and then passed inland.

By morning the floodwaters had begun to subside, but during that night of horror hundreds of homes had been completely demolished and thousands of people had been drowned or crushed to death in the destruction of their homes. We, however, passed the night in safety in the Wallis' home, and when we returned to our own, the only outward sign of damage was a tall chimney broken off at the roof line and many of the slate shingles ripped off the roof. The picture of damage inside, however, was much more heartbreaking; for when the shingles were ripped off there was nothing to prevent the recorded fourteen inches of rainfall from coming in. The plaster ceiling, both up-

4

and downstairs, soon gave way to the drenching rain; and floors, carpets, beds and other furniture were covered with a soggy, lime-caked mess.

Disposal of the more than eight thousand dead bodies was the first problem of the city government, and the initial solution was to load them on barges and tow them out to sea. Wind and tide, however, thwarted this plan and the corpses soon drifted back onto the beaches. It was then necessary to burn the bodies where they were found among the wreckage of shattered homes and buildings.

Sanitation for a city with broken water mains and a wrecked sewer system became a major problem. The city's water supply came from artesian wells at Alta Loma, nineteen miles across the bay from Galveston, but the storm had severed the lines where they crossed the bay between the mainland and Galveston Island. Fortunately, most homes in those days had cisterns for catching rainwater, as did my father's; but for this, the situation would have been much more serious.

Nevertheless, as the possibilities for an outbreak of typhoid, plague and other diseases became apparent, my father decided that it would be best to get the family out of Galveston as soon as possible until all cleanup operations were completed and sanitary conditions restored. Accordingly, arrangements were made for Mother and her four children, together with Aunt Tuncie and her daughter, Dorothy, to go stay with Uncle John at his farm in the community of Isaac, Virginia.

About a week after the storm of September 8, after being ferried across the bay to Virginia Point on the mainland (the railroad bridge not yet having been reconstructed) we boarded the train and departed for what was to be for us children a wonderful experience. Strangely enough, also, this long trip from Texas to Virginia was to record the

5

first event in my life which I can recall as pure memory. The very first occurred while our train was going slowly through a small town. On a track paralleling ours there stood an ancient locomotive which had a diamond-shaped smokestack. Locomotives of that vintage were scarce even in those days, and I suppose that the exclamations it brought forth from the members of our family were the reasons it became so indelibly fixed in my memory.

Eventually, this train arrived at the little station at Isaac. Uncle John met us with his carriage for Mother and my Aunt Tuncie and the two girls, while a wagon, driven by one of his Negro field hands, was to haul the family's trunks and other baggage and take my two brothers, John and Parker, out to the plantation. Here we were to stay for five months, or until cleanup operations at Galveston made it safe enough for us to return.

Chapter 2

Life on the Plantation

For the next five months John Griffin's farm was to be our refuge and our home. To a group of kids who had known nothing but city life, the experience for us was like moving into a new world.

After our huge trunks and other baggage had been brought up to the rooms assigned to us, Mother insisted on us helping with the unpacking and arrangement of our clothes in the chests and bureau drawers in order that the days and months ahead could proceed on a more orderly basis. But we could hardly wait to go downstairs and out into the yard to start exploring this wholly new environment.

When we were finally given our freedom by Mother, I can well imagine how that old antebellum house resounded to delightful squeals and yells that had not been heard within its walls for many a year, for Uncle John had never married. Out into the yard we dashed, and the first thing that caught our eyes was the orchard extending from the north side of the house with its trees loaded with red, ripe apples. Fruit such as this had been absent from our diet since the hurricane had struck two weeks before, so we climbed the fence and my older brothers got up into the branches of the trees and started tossing down to us some of the choicest specimens. Before we could fill our pockets there was an ominous sound of grunts and squeals and the clacking of rushing feet coming towards us. Glancing in that direction we saw a large number of pigs advancing, as we thought then, to attack us. My two brothers dropped from the trees and all of us scrambled up and over the rail fence to safety. Later, when we related how narrowly we had all missed being killed, Uncle John explained to us city-bred kids that pigs did not kill people, and that he had purposely had the pigs turned into the orchard so that they could feast on the apples which had fallen from the trees.

After dinner, which we soon learned was always served in the middle of the day, Uncle John took us down to the big barn where the cows and horses were housed during the bitter days of winter, and the hay which was to feed them had already been harvested and stored high above in the big loft. At the far end of the building he showed us into a room where he kept the carriage, some plows and other implements. There were several sets of harness suspended on the walls around the room. In one corner was a large stack of garden tools, rakes, hoes and shovels and two huge hemispheric iron kettles.

We left the big barn and started back toward the house. On the way Uncle John stopped at a small building and opened the door. The inside walls and ceiling were black, but from the light which entered the door, we could see hanging from the joists overhead many slabs of bacon and hams. We were told that this was the smokehouse. What was a smokehouse, we wondered. Uncle John pointed to the ashes on the dirt floor and explained that hickory logs were burned here so that the smoke from them would flavor and cure the hams and bacon hung above. The black objects above did not look very attractive to us at the time, but we later learned that we had never tasted any ham or bacon as delicious and as appetizing as these.

Nearby was a corncrib, and Uncle John showed us the difference between the regular corn which could be ground into cornmeal or shelled and fed to the chickens, and the smaller ears which were popcorn. Later, when cold weather came and fires were built in the fireplaces, we were allowed to help ourselves and enjoy the excitement of popping the corn over the red coals in the fireplace.

Close by was another small building and when the door was opened we practically gasped with amazement. It was filled from floor to ceiling with peanuts, and we were urged to fill our pockets and to help ourselves whenever we wanted. With the coming of winter we learned how to roast them by laying long rows of nuts on the hearth across the width of the fireplace.

As Uncle John continued to lead the way back to the big house we passed another building which the city-bred kids could recognize as the chicken house, and off to the right, back of the apple orchard, there was a row of four cabins where, Uncle John explained, the Negro field hands and their families lived. All the houses were alike: a brick chimney at one end and a slanting shed roof over the front porch.

Just before reaching the grape arbor which led into the lawn and flower gardens we passed the two-holer privy at

9

the back of the big house, and, from a faint odor we noticed in passing, we did not need to be told what this building was used for.

The next morning as we were finishing breakfast, Uncle John asked me if I would like to go with him to gather the eggs. I readily accepted and, taking my little hand in his, he led the way out to the chicken house. Inside there were bars across one end for the chickens to roost on, and along the back there was a row of box nests in which the hens laid their eggs. Uncle John started at one end of the row reaching under each hen and taking whatever eggs he found and put them gently into the basket he carried. Suddenly he stopped, for something on the floor, stretched out against the wall which supported the nests, had caught his experienced eye. I jumped behind Uncle John's leg and held on tightly, for there lay a brown snake about five or six feet long and as big around as a man's arm. At intervals of about a foot along its body were round bulges where it was still trying to digest the eggs taken from the nests. This was a chicken snake, Uncle John explained, and quite harmless to people, and he called to one of the Negro workers to come take it away. It was in such a stupor from its gorging of eggs that it offered no resistance when picked up. This was the first time I had ever seen a snake, and in spite of Uncle John's assurances, it was some time before my spirits began to calm and my fear left me.

With the approach of fall weather there was a noticeable chill to the air. Looking out the window one morning, I saw that the fields and outbuildings were covered with a white blanket of frost. Out in back of the house I could hear voices and occasionally the sound of Uncle John giving directions to the Negro help. When I went down to breakfast I asked the old Negro cook what was going on. "It's hog-killing time, honey!" she exclaimed

10

with a smile and a brightness in her eyes. "It's hog-killing time!"

Donning cap and jacket, I hurried down the path to an open area near the smokehouse where I found many of the Negro men and women being supervised by Uncle John. Long tables had been brought out, and hanging from a branch of the tree were the bodies of five or six hogs with their bellies slit open and all of the entrails piled on the long tables where the Negro women were selecting the choice parts, such as the livers and hearts. After they had been washed and laid aside, they proceeded to empty, wash and clean the long intestines which were to be used later for stuffing with sausage meat.

Nearby was a roaring fire, and Uncle John was busy cleaning a large iron kettle about four feet in diameter. This he did by first scouring the inside of the kettle with coarse granulated salt to remove any accumulation of rust and dirt. After this, it was thoroughly washed, set on the log fire and filled with water. When the water had come to a boil, a hog was taken down from the tree, thoroughly dipped into the hot water for a period just long enough to loosen its bristles, then hung from the tree branch where some of the workers scraped its body clean of all bristles. This operation was repeated until all six hogs had been denuded, and then brought, one at a time, to one of the long wooden tables where they were butchered and the hams and sides were selected to go into the smokehouse where a fire of hickory logs was slowly burning. Other portions of the animals were cut off and placed in big pans, later to be seasoned and ground into sausage meat and stuffed into the cleaned intestines. When completed, these too were hung up in the smokehouse for curing. During all the process of butchering, big chunks of excess fat had been sliced off, and these were later rendered into lard.

11

What a day of excitement this had been for us city-bred kids! While we had always had bacon for breakfast at our home in Galveston, and baked ham on occasion, the thought had never occurred to us to question where it came from. Though the day had continued bitter cold it was impossible for Mother to entice us away from this scene and all of the various operations involved in preparing these tasty items of hickory-smoked food which we were to enjoy many times during our stay.

A few days later the weather had warmed up and we spent much time outside, climbing the apple trees when we no longer feared the roaming pigs, and exploring the green pine forest beyond the cornfield. On one occasion, my oldest brother John, upon seeing my sister Margaret and her cousin Dorothy going into the privy, got a brilliant idea. Calling his brother Parker he suggested that they each get a long, thin twig, sneak up quietly behind the privy and poke the twigs through the wide cracks in the boards and tickle the bottoms of the two girls so as to make them think that spiders or snakes were attacking them. In no time at all the two girls ran screaming from the privy clutching their panties and dresses and running to the big house. As they ran, my brothers could contain themselves no longer and laughed in glee. Of course, the girls excitedly related to their mothers what had happened, and while my mother tried to make light of the incident as only a prank that the boys had pulled in order to give the girls a little scare, Dorothy's mother took the position that it was an immoral act and that my brothers should be punished severely. After much pressure and possibly because she realized that there would be little peace in the family, Mother gave in against her better judgment and proceeded to give John, the instigator of this foul plot, a sound spanking. Poor John was so mortified by the false stamp of immorality and the injustice of his punishment that he crawled as far back under the big double bed in his room as he could get and could not be coaxed out for the rest of the day.

With the advance of winter, Christmas eventually came to our temporary Virginia home. While I can remember that we had a Christmas tree, a shapely sapling from the nearby pine forest, and many small presents from Father back in Galveston and from other members of the family, the most vivid memory I have of the occasion is that when we awoke in the morning, the outside world was covered with snow, the first that I had ever seen. After breakfast and all presents had been opened, Mother gave in to our pleas and we were allowed to go out and experience for the first time this magic land of whiteness. I was still too young to participate in battles with snowballs, but when the excitement of this had subsided and someone suggested we make a snowman, I could participate with the older children with much enthusiasm.

The days and weeks went by rapidly. In addition to Uncle John, the household had another member for three months during the summer when school was not in session. This was his sister Aunt Julia, who taught in the public school at Franklin, about ten miles away, and who taught in the Baptist Sunday school there almost to the day of her death. She never married, and was a prim and straight-laced fundamentalist. She would allow no one to launder her clothes except the old Negro woman on the farm who had done it ever since Julia was a small girl; and so, each week the postman picked up a package from Amanda addressed to Julia and left one addressed for Amanda from Julia. During the summer vacation she would come home to keep house for Uncle John. As she managed to come home only two or three times while we were there we did not get to see much of her.

Spring was soon in the air, and on one bright day Mother decided it was time for her to visit the doctor in Franklin in order to have a checkup on her pregnancy which was now in about its seventh month. So, Uncle John had the old white horse hitched to the buggy, and, taking me with her simply to keep me out of the hair of the older children, Mother started to drive the short distance down the sandy road into Franklin. In addition to seeing the doctor we were charged with the responsibility of delivering to Aunt Julia her fresh laundry which Amanda had packed in an old suitcase and which now rested under my feet on the floor of the buggy.

And so we set out. Uncle John had assured Mother that old Whitey was very gentle, and all she had to do was follow the winding road and we would be in Franklin in thirty or forty minutes. It was a beautiful day with not a cloud in the sky, and though the air had the coolness of departing winter we were very comfortable with the lap robe covering our legs and feet. We passed a farm where sleek Jersey cows glanced up with unconcern at our approach, and from the trees on either side of the road there came the constant chatter and chirping of squirrels and birds in praise of the early return of spring. Suddenly the buggy jolted as if to stop and then lurched forward with all the speed old Whitey could muster. Mother strained and pulled back on the reins with all the strength she possessed but it had no effect. Clearly, this was a runaway, fraught with all the dangers I had heard tell about, and I held on to Mother tightly as the wild ride continued. A short distance ahead there was an abrupt turn in the road, and while I did not comprehend its danger I know now that Mother did, as she pulled with the last ounce of her strength on the reins and prayed silently for the protection of the baby she was carrying, for me and for her own safety.

14

And then it happened. As we reached the turn in the road with no reduction in old Whitey's speed, the buggy turned over on its side and Mother and I and the suitcase full of Aunt Julia's laundry were all catapulted out of the buggy onto the sandy road. Mother quickly sat up to survey the situation and found me crawling to her. I asked if she were hurt, and feeling no bones broken in either of us she suggested that we go over to the side of the road where we could sit on the grass. Old Whitey was nowhere in sight, but the suitcase which had contained Aunt Julia's fresh laundry had burst open and her clean dresses and her numerous unmentionables were scattered all over the road. We sat there for a few minutes while Mother tried to regain her composure and to assure herself that the accident had not triggered another accident with possibly more serious consequences.

We had not been there long before Mr. Holland, a neighbor of ours, drove up and stopped. Mother explained what had happened and asked if he would mind taking us back home. This he gallantly agreed to do and assisted Mother and me into his buggy. Then, picking up the battered old suitcase he proceeded to go all over the area picking up all of Aunt Julia's clothing and put the suitcase on the floor of the buggy.

It was not long before we were safe at home again, relating all of the harrowing details of the accident to the entire household. Two days later Uncle John drove mother into Franklin where the good doctor found nothing amiss. Later, however, when Aunt Julia was told of the accident and of how Mr. Holland had to gather up her laundry and repack the suitcase, her face flushed a deep pink and she exclaimed, "How could you have let him do that? Why, I have never been so embarrassed in all my life!"

Letters from Galveston reported much progress in repairing the damage caused by the storm, and sanitary conditions had been pronounced safe and almost back to normal. The inside walls of our home had all been re-plastered, the broken chimney rebuilt and the missing slate shingles replaced on the roof. As much as we kids would have liked to stay on the farm a little longer, Mother explained why we must terminate our visit. So, we began to pack our trunks and bags, and when the final days came for our departure for the long trip back to Texas, there were tears in the eyes of all.

Chapter 3

Early Years at Home

It was good to be back at our home once more for it was much like it was before the great storm had struck with such fury. All of the debris of broken tree limbs, slate shingles and brick had been cleared away. There had been little structural damage in our neighborhood since this area was so far from the gulf that it had not been subjected to the violent wave action which had destroyed so many homes nearer the beach.

We had not had a chance to see that devastated area yet, but when we went up to the second-floor porch which faced south we could hear something we had never noticed before. This was the constant roar of the surf over a mile away; and when we looked out of the attic windows we could see the horizon of the gulf and a narrow band of

17

blue water over the rooftops of the intervening houses. These changes, we soon learned, were due to the fact that while our house was on Avenue D, there was hardly a single house left standing between Avenue M and the old shoreline of the gulf. How lucky we felt we were!

Of course, there was much to do for all of us during the next few days. The other kids in the neighborhood flocked over to greet us the minute they knew we were home and listened with awe as we related some of our adventures in Virginia. Days passed before we, or Mother, felt that we were completely settled down again. There was still much to be done in getting new carpets and drapes installed and putting the house in order. With the help of the two Negroes, Becky and Anice, the former semblance of livability was restored, and, on May 15, Mother finally gave birth to a pretty little girl.

Our house was quite large as measured by architectural standards for a house of the average family of today, and we loved every inch of it. Rooms were larger, ceilings higher and porches, or galleries as they were called, were much more generous than one finds today. The ceilings on the first floor were twelve feet high, while those on the second floor were ten, and under the whole house there was a basement with six feet of head room. There were upper and lower galleries on the front of the house, and on the back, or south side, two broad, L-shaped galleries connected by an outdoor stair. These wide, covered galleries were wonderful places for the quieter forms of play, and, regardless of the weather, we spent many happy hours with our drawing, painting, playing school and running our mechanical trains and "making things," an almost constant diversion in our family. From the window of her room opening onto the upper gallery Mother was always

18

readily available for advice or help with some project of ours or to arbitrate some dispute.

One day, some years later, I happened to be in my father's office when he had a contractor there to discuss the possibility of raising the height of the balustrade of the upstairs front porch, as he felt that there was a possibility of one of us falling over. He had the architect's plans of the house spread out before them, and this was the first blueprint I had ever seen. When the contractor had left, Father showed me the full set of plans, explaining to me the floor plan, the various elevation plans, the roof plan and how they were all drawn to the same scale in order that the carpenters, masons, roofers and plumbers could build the house just as the architect had drawn it. The first floor plan showed a reception hall with a winding stairway to the second floor, a music room and living room separated by broad sliding doors on the left. The dining room on the right was separated from the kitchen by the butler's pantry. Opening onto the porch was a large pantry where groceries were stored.

The upstairs floor plan showed the master bedroom adjacent to the bathroom on the right of a hall which ran from the front gallery to the back gallery, and on the left side of the hall two large bedrooms. In a space above the storage pantry on the first floor was a small room labeled on the blueprint, "Trunk Room." This was a real necessity, for in those days, whenever anyone travelled, one or more trunks were always taken along, but when not in use there had to be a place to store them. Adjoining the trunk room with a door opening onto the gallery at the top of the outdoor stairway was another large room which the architect had designed on the blueprint as Servant's Room, but which was used by my two brothers, and in turn by me.

The two back galleries overlooked a yard which then

19

seemed to me as large as a circus lot, but today it appears to have shrunk in size and I can't help but wonder how we ever managed to carry out all of the various activities which took place during our childhood. In one corner there was a small servants' house which was occupied by the various servants until it was torn down and replaced by a stable and garage some years later. On the opposite side was a chicken house and run, and adjacent to the main house was an elevated cistern, the top of which extended almost as high as the roof. Except in time of emergency, such as that following the great storm, this was used only for laundering the clothes and watering the lawn and flowers. Later, after assurances of a permanent supply from the city mains, this entire structure was taken down and removed.

In the basement, one corner was reserved for the woodpile and kindling that was used for cooking and for starting the coal fire in the big stove in the downstairs hall in winter. The coal bin in another corner of the basement had two compartments; one had a capacity of one ton of anthracite or hard coal, and a smaller compartment which held several gunnysacks of charcoal needed by the washer woman who did the laundry. Beyond this was a toilet room for the use of the servants, and next to this was the darkroom which my father used in connection with his photographic hobbies. The rest of the basement, approximately three-fourths of the total area, was available to us children for duly authorized play space. It was always cool in summer down there and it made a wonderful place in which to build boats, pushmobiles and maintain a gymnasium. Our front yard was given over to lawns and flowers and, other than an occasional excursion in the lawn swing, we did little playing there.

Our house was located only four blocks from the wharves on the north side of the island, and the noises along the waterfront will always be vivid in my memory. Ships from all over the world docked there to load cotton and other cargo, and the screech of the winches and the brakes of the switch engines bringing new carloads of cargo to shipside went on all day. At Pier 14 stood the great grain elevator, and if there was any grain to be loaded, its loud whistle would be blown at seven in the morning, at noon and one at five o'clock in order to regulate the activities of the workmen. The whistles of tugboats in the harbor, and of great ships entering or leaving port could also be heard when there was a slight breeze from the north, and I often wondered from where they had come or to what far country they were sailing. At the foot of Sixteenth Street there was a marine ways where the snapper schooners, tugs and other small vessels could be hauled out of the water, have their bottoms scraped clean of marine growth, have their seams recaulked and given a fresh coat of paint. There is no other sound like that of a ship or barge being caulked — when we were playing on the upstairs front gallery or when the wind was out of the north, the "cleek, cleek, cleek" of the caulking mallets striking the chisels, driving the oakum into the seams, would be heard all day. Sometimes, when the breeze was blowing in a line from the marine ways to our house, one could actually smell the tarry odor of the oakum.

There were sights, too, as well as sounds and smells. We could see the tops of the masts of the steamers tied up at the wharves, and sometimes could distinguish their house flags and the flags of their nationality. There were also times when a ship had had a rough passage and would have to set flying all of the International Code signal flags to dry them out, and the ship then would have the appearance of being in full dress, as it is called in the navy. At that period steam had not fully replaced the sailing ship, and it was not unusual to see the tall masts and spars of a square-rigger above the roofs of the intervening houses between us and the harbor. Once, when I was about six years old, my mother called me to come up on the front gallery where she pointed out what was to us a thrilling sight. Over the rooftops were the masts and spars of the largest full-rigged ship we had ever seen, and standing on the yardarms in blue uniforms were rows of sailors preparing to make sail and get under way. The masts and spars had been scraped and varnished, and the shrouds and rigging stood out clearly. Soon, the ship slowly began to move out into the main channel and finally disappeared from view. Mother told us it was a navy training ship, probably the old *Constitution* after it was rebuilt, but of this I am not certain.

In our immediate neighborhood, that is, within a radius of three or four blocks, a number of well-to-do and socially prominent families had their homes. During the latter part of the nineteenth century and the early part of the twentieth when the immigration laws permitted the entrance of people from all over Europe to settle in central and western Texas, many large fortunes were made by some of these neighbors of ours by importing and wholesaling the supplies needed by this growing population of settlers in the interior of the state. Such supplies called for everything, from plows and coal to flour and sugar, in ever-increasing demand. Other people of note made their fortunes by selling the land on which these immigrants settled. Other family fortunes were made by engaging in banking and shipping. A half a block to the west of us was the tall-columned home of the Austins, descendants of people who had received large land grants from Mexico before Texas had won her independence. Two blocks to the east lived the Wilkins and the Fock families, still supplying the needs of the developing West. Next to the Wilkins lived the Runge family who owned large sheep ranches and whose five children were friends of mine.

Across the street from the Focks' lived Mrs. Rosenberg, the widow of the city's greatest philanthropist, having shared some of his accumulated wealth by giving the fine elementary school I was to attend, an orphans' home and a splendid public library to the city. Many afternoons Mrs. Rosenberg would go past our house seated in her beautiful victoria drawn by two sleek bays and driven by the coachman seated on his high seat in front. She always carried her little parasol, the top of which could be turned parallel to the handle when she wished to use it as a sunshade.

Next door to us lived a charming family, the Clarks, who had come from England many years ago, representing several British steamship lines. They still carried on the English custom of serving tea every afternoon at four o'clock, and while still very young I accompanied my mother on several of these occasions.

This, in brief, is the physical environment in which I spent much of my childhood. I can remember having no friends of my own age until I started to school, but with my sisters and brothers and their neighborhood friends I never lacked for company or playmates. For some reason, perhaps the initiative or inventiveness of my brothers, most of the neighborhood activities seemed to center in our backyard. These activities could have been anything from a game of hide-and-seek, tag or an amateur minstrel show. In the latter event we blackened our faces with burned cork, and with the help of Mother we fashioned costumes from old clothes. Banjos to plink were made from old cigar boxes, and bones to rattle were easy to come by from our friendly butcher, Mr. Meiners. Usually, the only inspiration we needed to start organizing a stage show was the sudden acquisition of a set of old roller shades whenever it became necessary to replace those in a particular room. By piecing these together and rolling them on a light pole the primary requirement of any theatre, the curtain, was ready at hand. Anyone not a member of the cast, which included our parents, was charged an admission fee of two cents. As a kid too little to have a part and by consequence of being a relative of the promoters, I was usually given the title of ticket taker or, sometimes, janitor — titles which made me feel as important as the stars.

On other occasions, a circus would be organized, and more pleasure would be obtained from the construction of the props than from the actual performance, it seemed to me. Orange crates with wooden bars nailed across the opening were used to house a neighbor's cat properly labeled "Man Eating Tiger," and in another cage a little fox terrier labeled "Mountain Lion." A trapeze and horizontal bar were erected on which my brothers performed. Of course, there was always one clown of sorts.

One day when I was about five years old, Father had some old timbers and boards from a building that was being demolished delivered to the house for the wood sawyer to cut and split into kindling. The wood sawyer was an elderly Negro who carried a folding buck, an axe and a bucksaw from house to house, and converted the four-foot lengths of oak cord wood into pieces of suitable size for the kitchen stove which had to be fired up three times a day. The old man would set up his buck, place a piece of wood across the notches of the buck, lubricate his saw with an eight- or ten-inch piece of bacon rind which he had wheedled from the cook and began sawing the logs into short chunks. When he had accumulated a pile three or four feet high, he would split the boards into halves and quarters by setting them upright and striking them with the sharp blade of his axe. Kindling, of course, was needed to start the oak to burning, and this came from crates, boxes or old lumber.

Among the lumber that was delivered that day were a number of long 2" x 12" yellow pine floor joists and a piece of 6" x 6" about eight feet long, and this was all that was needed to give my brother John the idea that we needed a merry-go-round. He planted the 6" x 6" upright in a deep hole and drove a heavy spike in the center of the top. Then, drilling a hole in the center of one of the large boards, he slipped this over the spike in the post and we had a new form of entertainment. With a kid seated on each end of the board and another to start it revolving in a circular motion we had some rare thrills. All went well for several days. Now it was my turn to ride again, and with one of the neighborhood boys intent on establishing a new speed record, the spike suddenly came loose and the board and I flew off into a crazy orbit. The boy on the opposite end of the board escaped with only a rolling tumble, but I came down to earth with the heavy plank across one leg. At first I could not move and everyone, especially I, thought my leg was broken and I was carried upstairs to my bed to await the arrival of old Dr. Randall. Fortunately, there were no broken bones, but it was several days before I could begin to hobble around. When the doctor had left, my brother John came up to my bed to tell me how sorry he was, and taking my hand, he slipped his jackknife into it. This act of tenderness I later learned was typical of John all through life where the suffering of little kids was concerned. It brought tears to my eyes and I tried to assure him that he should not feel any blame for the accident.

When I was a kid there was a frequently occurring

event which always aroused a feeling of mystery and wonder. These were the funeral ceremonies then prevalent. There were no privately operated funeral chapels such as we have today and the services were generally conducted at the home of the deceased or at the church or both, followed by a slow parade to the cemetery.

Scores of raggedly dressed children congregated outside the place where services were being conducted, mutely waiting for the priest to come out, followed by the pall bearers bearing the casket of the deceased. It was then loaded into a glass-enclosed hearse drawn by a team of horses. Against the curb for some distance down the street were empty horse-drawn carriages, known then as hacks, which were rented for the occasion from the undertaker, to transport the relatives and other mourners to the church or to the cemetery. These were large, black vehicles with a door on each side and two cushioned seats facing each other and equipped with hard rubber tires, the epitome of luxurious transportation. The driver sat out in the open on a high seat in front directing a team of sleek horses. As the hearse slowly drew away these hacks advanced and were filled with members of the family and prominent friends. Other mourners fell in behind the last carriage and joined the procession on foot. Frequently, for a person of distinction in his group, a brass band would be engaged to lead the procession, mournfully playing Chopin's "Funeral March" over and over again as it marched the long distance to the church or cemetery, and many times as we kids were playing on our upper gallery we could hear the doleful music slowly approaching faintly from afar, then growing louder as it passed and finally fainting away into the distance as it moved on.

Our parents never permitted us to attend any of these funeral services nor the interment in the cemetery, but the solemnity of what we could see and hear left strong impressions of the mystery of death and its apparent importance as the end of life. Notwithstanding our Presbyterian upbringing, we kids attached little religious significance to the only part of the funeral service we had witnessed, but until we had grown quite a bit older we always enjoyed giving any pet dog or cat that had died in the neighborhood a proper funeral such as we knew it. A suitable box was found for a casket and with the pet's body inside, it was hauled in one of our little wagons. The rest of the kids strung out in a long procession to a secluded corner of the yard where it was interred and grave markers, suitably inscribed, placed at the head and foot.

I have mentioned the supply of charcoal which was always kept on hand for laundering the clothes. This was an event which took place every Monday morning provided it was not raining, in which case the job was postponed until the next fair day, for it was a sizable task to maintain clean clothes for a large family, to say nothing of the sheets, pillowcases and table linen. As soon as we had all finished breakfast, Becky and her helper went through the house gathering up all the soiled items and packing them into large baskets which they proceeded to carry down to the backyard where they had the copper wash boiler already set up on bricks. Here the contents of the baskets would be sorted into three piles, white, colored and woolen. Each would receive different treatment, but in accord with long-established standards. A fire had been started under the copper boiler, now filled with cistern or rain water. As the water grew hot Becky would take a huge bar of laundry soap and cut shavings and let them fall into the water and dissolve. Then the clothes were dumped in, stirred around and punched and prodded with a laundry stick, the top half of an old broomstick. After being well

27

boiled in the sudsy water, the laundry was lifted piece by piece and transferred to a large galvanized tub filled with warm water. Inside this tub was a corrugated brass washboard on which each piece of linen or clothing was spread, thoroughly soaped and rubbed up and down until clean and ready to be transferred to another tub filled with rinse water; then it was put into a third tub into which bluing had been added to accentuate the whiteness of the wash. The dresses and other pieces which would require starch were treated separately and all pieces were wrung as dry as possible then hung on ropes strung all over the yard, for drying in the sun. With the wash all fastened to the ropes with wooden clothespins, each line was adjusted to a proper height by the use of clothesline poles so as to keep the clean laundry from contact with the ground. These were eight to ten feet long with a point on one end and a V notch on the other so that it could engage the rope. After an hour or two in the sun, the dry laundry was taken down and packed into the large wicker baskets and placed inside Becky's quarters. When this part of the job was finished, the boiler and the tubs would be washed out and hung up in the basement, the clothespins gathered up and placed in a sack, the clotheslines taken down and the boiler wash stick and clothesline poles carefully stowed in the basement so as to be readily available for the next week.

The next day, rain or shine, the second phase of the laundering began. This took place in Becky's quarters where two ironing boards were set up with a sheet-iron-covered clay brazier placed between them. A charcoal fire was soon glowing red, on which five or six heavy flatirons were placed. Linens were selected from the wicker basket and spread out on the ironing boards, and the two Negresses were ready to start work. A warm or partially heated iron will not press, and before beginning to attack the work

28

spread out on the ironing boards, an iron was taken from the brazier and its temperature was properly tested. This was done by wetting one's finger in the mouth and touching it gently to the bottom of the iron. If it "sizzled," the iron was hot enough; it was then wiped on a cloth pad at the end of the ironing board and if there was no indication of scorching, it was safe to begin ironing the clothes. This procedure had to be followed through the day, and by rotating the irons as they lost sufficient heat, they were replaced on the brazier and a hot iron selected.

This work might go for two full days but the women did not seem to mind as long as there was companionship. As each piece was finished it was properly folded and placed carefully in the wicker baskets. There was much talk and gossip passing between the two women and it was from overhearing some of this that I received the first impression I had ever had that all people or families were not regarded alike. I was playing in the sand just outside Becky's window when I heard her say with some emphasis, "Well, that gal you just mentioned may be all right but she shore do work for some poor white trash. Now, me, I ain't never worked for nobody but quality folks, and I ain't never going to! You take the people I work for, they's all right, they's quality folks. They takes care of the niggers that works for them, and they always have, and you don't see them messing around with anybody but quality folks. No, sir!" These comments set me to thinking. I had never realized the different social strata, a possible carry-over from the days before the Civil War, and this new revelation was something I should have discussed with my mother. It was a fit subject for our dinner table discussions, but I was too timid to bring it up. As I grew older and knew what it meant I began to understand.

About the time I entered high school the problem of

securing domestic help became more and more difficult and we eventually began to patronize the commercial laundries, but I don't think my mother ever admitted that their laundry work was as clean as that which had been done on our own place where the chores were on a well-organized basis.

The size of the family made it necessary for each of us to carry as much of his load as possible, and it would be unthinkable for us to go to Sunday school without freshly polished shoes. Each child was expected to see that this chore was carried out by himself each Saturday night. There was never any fussing or whining about carrying out such assigned tasks for we were a well-disciplined group and whenever our parents established any routine tasks such as these we knew beyond any question that they had to be done.

Another thing which added much in the way of the smoothness and order in our daily life was the fact that we always sat down to meals as a family group. This was not easily accomplished, particularly at breakfast with only one bathroom to accommodate a family of our size. Many times it seemed impossible to leave our play and get washed up in time to be seated at dinner before having to undergo the questioning eyes of my father. The dinner table discussions which took place were always most interesting. At breakfast Father would always scan through the morning paper, sharing with us any items of importance and giving us the benefit of his opinions regarding such events. At dinner, in the middle of the day, if conversation seemed to lag, Mother would ask, "Well, did you run across any of our friends today?" And Father would say, "Oh, yes. Julius dropped in to say hello. Hedwig has a bad chest cold, but Dr. Randall didn't think it was anything serious." And Mother would say, "Oh, that's too bad.

Maybe I had better drop by to see her." Then my sister Margaret might relate some incident that happened at school which brought on a discussion between all as to the fairness or injustice of the matter. Sometimes there would be discussions of political aspirants or present office holders, or of events of a questionable nature which had occurred in local, state or national government, and it was from the discussion of these matters that we all learned to demand integrity and intelligence in our government officials and office seekers. My father was particularly fond of President Taft, perhaps because they were both natives of Ohio. One time he wrote the president inviting him to come down to Galveston for a fishing trip. He received a gracious acknowledgement, but of course the president could not accept. Projects we kids had planned or were under way in the backyard were discussed occasionally, primarily to get Father's approval while all of us were present to put the pressure on, should he have any objections. Usually there would be none, provided we did our assigned chores of mowing the lawn, or in winter, keeping the coal scuttles filled. Before ending our dinner table discussions there would always be a reminder from Mother for any of us who might have music or dancing lessons for that afternoon. During all the years of these dinner table discussions we children received much good counsel as to our conduct such as respect for the religious views of others and the need to respect the feelings as well as the property rights of all people, and to be honest at all times.

At breakfast as each of us finished and had packed our lunch for school we went to Father as he was finishing his second cup of coffee and kissed him good-bye. I never quite understood the necessity for this ritual show of affection any more than I did the requirement that when Father came home at noon and in the evening we were all supposed to drop whatever we were doing and rush down to the front door and greet him with another kiss. But I am sure Father enjoyed these little attentions no matter how routine or habitual they became in time. And then, of course, there was the good-night kiss. We all loved Father deeply, but as the practice soon lost its spontaniety we soon learned to accept it as a duty, and did not even discuss it among ourselves.

When I was five or six years old we were surprised to see the Wells Fargo Express Company's wagon delivering a large heavy box to our house. It was addressed to Father. The shipping label showed only that it had come from Cincinnati, and we could hardly wait for Father to come home from work to see what the box contained. When he finally arrived and removed the cover he took out a heavy, square object with a round turntable on top. Other items were brought out, including a conical-shaped horn, a small crank which fitted into the side of the mysterious box, a diaphragm with a small hole for admitting a bright steel needle, of which there were a hundred or more in a small envelope, and ten or twelve black disks, each with a different name printed in gold letters. When Father got all the parts assembled he placed one of the black disks on the turntable, set the needle attached to the diaphragm and horn on the outer edge of the black disk and released the starter lever. After the disk had revolved once or twice beautiful music began to issue from the horn. We all sat transfixed; it was the first phonograph we had ever seen or heard. After a moment we all began to exclaim how wonderful it was but before we could get started, Father commanded silence, just as he would have done had the artist actually been present in person.

At the end of the recording father explained that this was a gift to all the family from his cousin Robert, and

32

that we should always treat the instrument carefully so that we could get the most enjoyment from it. Among the dozen records, I can now recall only a few of them: a part from the opera *Martha,* another from *Samson and Delilah,* and a xylophone recording, as well as a piano and several orchestral pieces. As time went on I learned to sing the melody of all these pieces and would often do so when playing alone in my sandpile out in the backyard. By trilling my tongue I could even reproduce the xylophone recording to perfection.

Father's insistence on complete silence during any musical rendition was explained to us as a courtesy we owed not only to the artist but to other listeners. This came up several times at our dinner table discussions, as did the matter of our general behavior in public. My sisters were particularly cautioned against laughing loudly: a *lady* never should be guilty of this. During one of these discussions my older sister reported that one of her teachers had stated that "a loud laugh displays a vacant mind," and the discussion which followed made its meaning clear to us.

Chapter 4

I Visit Father's Boyhood Home

One night after we had finished supper and were seated as usual in the living room, Father announced that he would like to visit some scenes of his boyhood. We all fell silent and waited for we knew from experience that he rarely ever expressed a desire to do something until he had already made up his mind to do it. We knew, of course, that he had been born and brought up in Cincinnati, and to us kids that was a long, long way off. Although he had an older sister and some cousins still living there he had been back only once, many years ago when he had taken his mother's remains back home to be buried in beautiful Spring Grove Cemetery.

While we waited expectantly, Mother broke the silence by saying, "Well, I think that would be fine for you. You need a rest and the children and I can get along perfectly all right while you are gone."

"Oh, no," said Father, "you are going with me!" He went on to explain that since he had taken John and Parker on his trip to New York the year before, they could stay at Grandma's, and that Mother, the girls and I were to go with him. Well, just as we had thought, he had it all planned!

My sisters and I were quite thrilled over the idea of our making this long trip, and the days ahead were busy ones getting what new clothes we needed, getting older ones mended and missing buttons replaced. Two trunks were moved from the trunk room into the house where they could be filled more conveniently, along with a suitcase and a satchel for carrying the bare necessities we would need en route. Father, of course, had to arrange for the train tickets and Pullman reservations, while even Aunt Martha had been busy up in Cincinnati finding a place where we could stay which would be close to her apartment. This she did, securing comfortable rooms in a private home, the owners of which later treated us as their guests rather than their tenants.

Although we kids never thought it would, the day of departure finally came. We had told our friends good-bye and about two hours before train time, a horse-drawn open truck came to get our trunks and take them down to the express company at the station. There they would remain until Father presented his tickets and had them checked in, after which they would be loaded into the baggage car. About an hour after our trunks had left the house a hack from the livery stable, there being no such thing as a taxi cab in those days, came to transport us down to the Union Station. We all waited until Father had checked the trunks and verified our Pullman reservations and then boarded the train. In a few minutes we could hear the conductor shouting, "All aboard!" After another minute or two while a late arrival hastened to get aboard we felt a slight jerk to the train and were then gliding smoothly out of the long station.

By the time we had crossed the bay on the long wooden trestle it was beginning to get dark and we could no longer watch the scenery speedily passing by. So we began to amuse ourselves by watching the porter make up the berths. As we had had a light supper just before leaving home we did not respond to the call of the white-jacketed waiter from the dining car announcing, "First call to dinner!" as he passed through the train. However, when we were all washed and dressed the next morning we went into the diner and had a delightful breakfast while speeding through forests and farmlands.

Most of the day was spent in watching the scenery go by as we wound through hills and sped over many bridges that spanned the creeks and small rivers. As we came to many towns along our route, the train would stop at the larger ones to take on or discharge a few passengers, but at the small towns it raced through without slackening speed. The small stations were all very much alike with a waiting room, ticket office and baggage room inside and a semaphore signal tower and two or three hand trucks on the platform paralleling the tracks. As we went through these towns we could always hear the staccato ringing of the crossing warning bells and always marvelled at the weird change in pitch of the sound as we approached and then zoomed away. It would be years later before we would learn in our high school physics course the reason for this change in pitch of the warning bells.

It was on this trip that we learned how the mail was distributed by the railroads throughout the country. Each

36

passenger train included a mail car in which sacks of mail for the towns along its route were stored. Whether the train stopped or not these sacks would be tossed out onto the platform at a particular town by the mail clerk. To take on board any outgoing mail where the train was not scheduled to stop, the sack of mail was suspended vertically between two steel arms extending close to the track. Regardless of the speed of the train the mail clerk had only to extend a large steel hook and the suspended sack was snatched from its supporting arms and brought up to the open door of the mail car. Here the sack would be opened and the mail sorted into other sacks according to the destination indicated and these sacks would be thrown onto the platform of the appropriate station as we speeded by. By watching from an open window we could occasionally see the mail clerk snatch the suspended sack and we were thrilled to see with what ease and precision this task was performed.

At long intervals along the way the engine would have to stop beside a huge water tank to replenish the water used in the boiler for making steam. The engineer would carefully stop opposite a large pipe hinged to the tank. When this was pulled down water would flow into the engine's tank, and we would soon be under way again.

That night after dinner we arrived at a large city, whose name I have now forgotten, and pulled into a long station. The porter told us that we would be here for a few minutes in order that a new engine could be coupled on to take us the rest of the way. Father came in from the vestibule where he had been chatting with the conductor and told Mother he was going to the newsstand in the station for a newspaper and some cigars, but would be right back. After a few moments there was a slight jerk to our car and the chugging sound of an engine moving away from us. We now sat silently in the smoky gloom of the station waiting for the new engine to be coupled on when, suddenly, there was a jarring crunch, and the next instant our car was being speedily pulled out of the station. Thinking that we were again on our way to Cincinnati our hearts were gripped with panic! Father had been left behind. We were almost at the point of tears as we realized the seriousness of our situation. Why, Father had all our tickets, our baggage checks and, of course, the money we would need to pay for our meals! We looked appealingly at Mother who tried to reassure us and told us not to worry. Then, our car stopped almost as suddenly as it had been jerked out of the station and, as suddenly, began to back into the station again. We looked frantically out the windows to find Father to let him know where we were, but saw that we had backed in on an entirely different track and realized with renewed fright that he would never be able to find us now. At that moment there was another jarring crunch as our car was coupled onto another train, and we heard the chugging noise of the engine rapidly pulling away. All was quiet and still now and we just sat there for what seemed like hours, not knowing what fate had in store for us without Father. We were about as miserable as little kids can get, and nothing that Mother said seemed to make any difference. The minutes dragged by, each one seeming to make the outlook bleaker and bleaker. I got out of my seat so as to get closer to Mother, and, happening to glance down the aisle, I saw Father approaching with his newspaper in one hand and a box of candy for us in the other!

Compared to Galveston, Cincinnati was a metropolitan city even in those days. The downtown section was particularly impressive. Streetcars were everywhere, it seemed, and huge trucks pulled by strong percheron and clydesdale horses fought their way through traffic. The people crowding the sidewalks all seemed to be in a hurry to get somewhere. Adding to the noise were numerous newsboys hawking their wares which I discovered sold for only two cents. In one section of the city there was an open market offering all of the vegetables and fruits in season, and I was quite surprised to find that such things as beans and peas had already been shelled and could only be purchased in this way. Everything was fresh and clean, and we used to buy the various species of berries and ripe, red tomatoes which had a much more delicious flavor than I had ever tasted in Texas.

At that time the Ohio River still carried a large volume of freight in the stern-wheel and side-wheel river steamboats. One day Father asked me if I would like to go look at the river where he used to go swimming when he was a boy. We left the girls at home with Mother and Aunt Martha and set out. When at last we got to the river there, up at her dock, was the largest and most beautiful river steamer I had ever seen, the *Island Queen*. She was painted white all over except where gold leaf had been used to accentuate some of the carved wood filigree and for her nameboards on each side. There was a trickle of smoke coming from her two, tall smokestacks, and on each side of the hull the largest paddle wheels I had ever seen. To me she was a beautiful ship. Father said she had been a famous passenger ship, running regular schedules up and down the river, to Pittsburgh and even to St. Louis, but at this time she was being used for sight-seeing excursions. We went aboard, and after a few minutes, I heard the mighty blast of her whistle and noticed that we were slowly moving out into the stream and gathering speed as the huge paddle wheels turned faster and faster.

Father led me inside where the luxurious furnishings

and the mahogany panelling with its soft satin polish gave me the feeling I was in the palace of a wealthy and powerful king. As we moved on through, passing long rows of now unused cabins, we came to a place where we could look down into the engine room; huge pistons moved up and down turning the cranks on the shafts of the great paddle wheels.

The next day Father wanted to visit Spring Grove Cemetery where his mother and father and other members of the family were buried. Compared to the only cemeteries at Galveston, this was a marvel of beauty with immaculately kept lawns, gravel walks and flower gardens. Father showed me the grave markers where his father and mother were buried and read their names and explained the dates to me.

We did not stay very long and then set out to visit the city's Botanical Garden. This was even more beautiful than the cemetery. There were thousands of different species of flowering trees and shrubs; and the walks were outlined with meticulously trimmed hedges of red, green and yellow leafed plants not more than six inches high. The lily pools were filled with blooming species of all kinds, but the one which impressed me the most was one with a circular leaf three or four feet in diameter, the outer edge of which turned up vertically for three or four inches like a huge pan floating on the surface of the water. I was told that these could support the weight of a small child without sinking, but, of course, none of us ventured to test this.

Father tried to make our visit as educational as possible for us and arranged tours through some of the factories and industries. Two I shall never forget. The first was the famous Rookwood Pottery where we saw these beautiful pieces from a lump of clay through the drying, firing, painting and glazing processes, and for several years after we returned home, we would make vases, pitchers and bowls whenever we could obtain any clay. The other factory that left a lasting impression was where fine cut glass was made. I can recall how the artists would paint the design on the glass in thin red lines. When dry these pieces went to the cutting room where there were numerous bevel-edged grinding and polishing wheels on long tables or benches. By holding the glass on the rapidly turning bevel wheels it would be slowly moved as the wheel cut into the glass in conformity with the design. This required great skill, and it was time-consuming work, but the factory turned out hundreds of beautiful pieces a day.

A few days before we were to start back home Father asked me if I would like to attend a county fair. I had no idea what a county fair was, but readily assented and we were soon on our way. It seemed like we rode for many miles on the streetcar, finally crossing one of the great bridges across the river and landing in Kentucky. At the fair grounds we took in all the usual sights, but the features which impressed me the most were the horse races. We obtained good seats up in the grandstand and after we had witnessed two races with saddle horses, the sulky races started! A horse was hitched to a light, two-wheeled sulky without floor or sides. The driver was seated over the axle with his legs spread wide and his feet hooked into a leather strap on each shaft. This kind of racing was very exciting; there were a couple of spills on the turn, and one time the wheel of one sulky engaged that of another and the foul resulted in quite a set-to out on the track.

A few days later we said good-bye to our friends and relatives and boarded the train for the long trip back to Texas. One afternoon I ventured into the smoking room where my father and two other gentlemen were discussing the recent occurrence of a train robbery, and I was surprised to hear for the first time that Father had once experienced an unsuccessful attempt at such a crime. The engineer had refused to heed the warning signal of the robber gang to stop the train and instead continued at top speed. The frustrated robbers then began firing their pistols at the passing train and Father recounted how he could hear the sound of the bullets ricochetting between the double flooring of the Pullman car in which he had been riding. No one was hurt. Needless to say, however, when I retired to my berth that night I had great difficulty in getting to sleep, expecting at any moment to feel the train come to a stop and to hear the pistol shots of a gang of train robbers.

Chapter 5

What School Was Like

By the time I was old enough to start school the city was in the midst of a huge construction program designed to protect life and property from any future hurricanes. The plan called for a concrete sea wall seventeen feet high around the eastern and southern sides of the city and filling in behind this with sand dredged from the floor of the gulf. As the wall progressed westward, a canal, starting at the harbor, was dug parallel to it in order that the hydraulic dredges could come in from the gulf and discharge their cargoes of sand. The dredge boat would stop in the canal at a selected place where huge steel pipes would be connected and she would begin to pump out her cargo of sand and water. The sand quickly settled to the desired grade and the water ran off to the bay. Then pipes had to be constantly shifted so as to distribute the fill where needed.

The entire operation of dredging and filling required a large influx of laborers of an unusually low social order. In order to be convenient to boarding the dredge as they entered the canal, these families rented the small prefab, or commissary houses as they were called, in the east end of the city near the waterfront.

As there was only one elementary school serving the eastern part of the city, the children from these families necessarily had to attend the same school that I was to attend, a bitter problem as we shall see later.

In the fall after my seventh birthday I was duly enrolled in the low first grade at Rosenberg School. Here I met a few children who were to become my close companions for the rest of my life in Galveston. From grade to grade we were to remain together until we were graduated from high school in the same class. This group of about ten children were all from prominent families and of the same social strata as our own, and until I left to go off to college I never lacked having the staunchest of friends. As we became acquainted the boys naturally gravitated to our backyard, and as soon as school was out each day our yard began to fill. The game of cops and robbers had not come into being, but that of cowboys and Indians occupied much time, and the romance of being pirates was always appealing to such a group.

One afternoon while playing cowboys and Indians I had the role of a horse thief and was, of course, captured. With a rope around my neck the boys were dragging me across the lawn towards a tree when my sister Virginia came from the side of the house expecting to see my head separated from my body at any moment. With tears streaming down her face she rushed at the boys flailing her little fists and commanding them to stop before they succeeded in killing me. The boys stopped pulling on the rope immediately, not knowing whether to take to their heels or to burst out in laughter. I was struck by this show of loyal devotion and love on Virginia's part; indeed, I had never dreamed that she could have cared so much for me and I never forgot it. But what she did not know was that I was never for one moment in danger of losing my life, for I was being dragged along on my chest with forearms held close to my sides; the fingers of both hands were up under my chin so that they, rather than my neck, took the pull of the rope. When I arose and took the rope from around my neck it took some time to comfort her and assure her that I had not been hurt.

As we grew older, baseball consumed much of our time, and if there were not enough to make up two full teams we played a variation which was called One Eye Jim Bats. This might well have been called progressive baseball, for each prospective player shouted the position he wanted to start at, the number one spot, of course, being "batter" which was usually won by the biggest and loudest boy, with "catch," "pitch," "first," "second," etc. following in rapid order. If the batter succeeded in making a base hit, all players advanced to the next highest position, the catcher now becoming batter, the pitcher becoming catcher, and so on. If the batter made a home run he was privileged to bat again; if he were put out, all players advanced and the ex-batter started at the bottom at third base. It was a good game and afforded everyone some experience in playing all positions.

There were other games such as tin can hockey, and gymnastics on the horizontal bar and the trapeze in our backyard; and during the summer we spent much time swimming in the surf. One or two of the boys would come by my house after lunch, and after donning our swimming suits we would run a mile and a quarter down Fourteenth Street to the gulf where we would spend the rest of the afternoon trying to outswim, outduck and outrun each other. Why at least one of us never drowned will always be a mystery.

In addition to those I had met at school who were to become my lifelong friends I also met quite a few boys who were to be my constant enemies, and who were to provide many hours of misery and fear. These were the offspring of the dredge boat and pipeline workers who, without doubt, were the dregs of humanity. These kids had been taught to lie, to steal, to cheat and to curse and swear as well as their parents. I had not been in school but a few days when I knew all of the four-letter words and many more, most of them picked up when hurled in scorn at me and my friends. Since I had never heard such words used around our home, I knew instinctively that I was never to repeat them in the presence of any members of my family or friends. It was impossible to maintain peaceful status with them. In order to secure protection I tried to remain near the teacher who had the recess duty assignment. Since I lived thirteen blocks from school it was quite a different matter when school let out for the day, for there was no protective teacher except on rare occasions, and many times I was forced to run all the way home, or, if I were lucky, sometimes I could beat them to my friend Gig's house. The big trouble was that, first, they outnumbered us good kids, and, second, they had never heard of the Marquis of Queensberry rules; so it was not uncommon for ten or twelve of them to jump on two or three of us, particularly if their man who started the attack seemed to be getting the worst of it. There was no reason for the animosity on their part, for we had done nothing to hurt them in any way; they needed no reason

46

and sometimes fought among themselves. We learned that they were organized into two gangs, the Twelfth Street Gang and the Tenth Street Gang, and whenever warfare broke out between them, usually on Sundays, everything went — fists, rocks, bottles and knives. These little differences, however, did not prevent them from joining forces if they should find one or more of my friends on the street. Two of their members were expelled from school during my enrollment there, and two others achieved distinction later by winning for themselves long sentences in the State Penitentiary at Huntsville.

The public schools of Galveston rated high scholastically and a certificate of graduation from high school would admit one to almost any university in the country. Measured by the standards of that day this was all well and good, perhaps, but looking back to the many hours of boredom fills me with disgust and regret at the tremendous loss of time. Arithmetic, for example, was taught as a craft for future storekeepers, clerks and insurance people rather than as groundwork for the higher branches of mathematics we encountered when we entered high school. And the repetitious working of problems of the same kind, any one of which would have been sufficient to teach the principle involved, engendered in me a hatred for what could have been a very interesting subject. There was no such thing at that time as the new math which has proved so puzzling to many parents of the present space age. The absence of this kind of approach prevented us from realizing what a really beautiful discipline mathematics could be.

In English there was a composition assignment every week. This would have been splendid had there been any critique or discussion of our efforts to express our thoughts, and our organization of them. Our papers came back to us with a grade mark, and that was all.

47

We also had in English a book titled *Memory Gems*, which was an anthology of the poetry popular at the turn of the century. Every two weeks a poem was assigned to us to memorize and be able to recite in class. If a pupil could recite the poem line by line without error he received an *A;* if there were any stumbling or a line omitted, one stayed after school until it could be recited without error. It seems very doubtful whether the hundreds of hours spent on this effort improved our ability to use the English language or to even appreciate what might have been in the poet's mind when he set down his thoughts in meter and rhyme.

I enjoyed the course in geography for it took me away from this otherwise drab existence to far lands and seas and rivers all over the world. Geography was the earth, something you could get your teeth into, places you dreamed of going to someday, and it was something linked closely to history.

History, too, was taught not to bring out the great events of the past, what caused them and what effect they had on our civilization, but primarily as a means to test one's ability to memorize dates, names and places. No effort was made to correlate in time events which happened in one part of the world with those which took place in another or what effect one had on the other. And so, history as then taught was dull and wholly lacking in the interest which would have been generated in our youthful minds, had it been taught objectively.

At the time I started to school, I began taking piano lessons, as had my brother and sisters. Because of my father's great love for music and because he believed strongly in the thought that music was a necessary part of our cultural development he saw to it that each of his children had the opportunity to learn to play the piano.

48

An aptitude test, had any such thing been available in those days, would have saved him many hundreds of dollars, for certainly I had no aptitude or talent for the piano and actually lacked the physical coordination so necessary. Twice a week I went to my teacher's home where, for one hour, I tried to develop some ability, in addition to which I had to practice at home for one hour each day during school and two hours a day during vacations. These practice hours were mandatory and if I failed to put them in before Father came home from the office, then I had to do it under his critical eye and ear. After the end of the three years, my father was not happy with the results and secured a male teacher. For two more years this went on before Father realized that I had no talent and regretfully allowed me to stop. Of course, I did learn to play many pieces, but it was all memory work, note by note, bar by bar, and there was never any assurance that I could ever finish a piece without striking at least one foul note. This was as disappointing to me as it was to Father, for I really loved music and got much happiness from the choral singing at school and from the concerts and operas which I frequently attended.

Whenever a real artist or grand opera came to Galveston Father always saw to it that we attended the performance and I remember well hearing Sarah Bernhardt, Walter Damrosch and his orchestra, Paderewski, the operas *Il Trovatore* and *Carmen,* and that fantastic production of Rostand's *Chanticler.* In those days too, the black face minstrels were popular and acceptable, and I attended several of the best on circuit. When good stage plays would come to Galveston we got to see a number of these, among which I vividly recall *Rip Van Winkle, Little Lord Fauntleroy* and *The Roundup,* a thrilling western. Before we had local movie theatres, some feature films just perfected

49

by the budding movie industry came to Galveston for showing at the Opera House. One of the greatest of these which we saw was *The Great Train Robbery,* now considered a classic.

Then, too, there were the annual appearances of the great circuses which we always saw and enjoyed. The German circus, Hagenbeck, would tour America, but I think we got our biggest thrills from Ringling Brothers and the Barnum and Bailey circuses. These would always schedule a parade in the downtown section of the city. This would consist of the red and gilt animal cages led by the band and followed by great elephants and clowns and ending with the steam calliope. These free parades, which would be all that many poor people would see of the circus, were considered of such educational value by the school board that the schools were authorized to dismiss all pupils in time for them to go see it.

About two years after I started taking music lessons I had to start taking dancing lessons as did all of the boys and girls in our set. The school was held in the large auditorium of the Sacred Heart School and here I spent one afternoon of each week during the fall, winter and spring for several years. The teacher was a true classicist if ever there was one, and, no doubt, spent many frustrating moments trying to teach us the minuet, the schottische, the polka, the waltz and a number of Spanish, Russian and Greek folk dances. Interspersed between all these we were given lessons in ballroom etiquette and courtesy. Each year our teacher would go abroad for study during the summer, and the school would close with a big pageant to which the parents were invited. I can recall how my mother labored each year making several foreign costumes for the part I had to play, and how I hated every moment of it all.

By present-day standards we had very few toys except those we made. The modern electric railroad trains had not been invented, but we did have mechanical train sets whose motive power was supplied by a clockwork spring motor which had to be wound up every few minutes.

Another manufactured toy we had was called a magic lantern, which was a crude projector. The first one we had was operated by a small kerosene lamp, and the glass slides which came with it were one inch wide and six inches long with five or six colored pictures applied to the glass by some decal process. These slides were inserted between the lens and the lamp, having to be pushed along, pausing a moment at each fuzzy picture, and then inserting another slide. A white sheet had to be hung up to serve as a screen, and sometimes we would arrange the chairs in two rows in front of the sheet and put on a show for the other kids in the neighborhood. After we had exhibited the six or eight slides which came with the machine the whole thing became rather boring and it was impossible to attract any future spectators, until a few years later when my brother Parker received a much larger magic lantern with slides two inches wide and an electric light. Business then picked up.

A toy that we used to make ourselves was called a lantern box. These would range in size from an ordinary shoe box to large shirt or blanket boxes. The making of these gave free range to individual creative imagination and ability. On the sides and ends of the box we would draw pictures of dragons, or of the devil with horns and forked tail, or, in some cases, of a ship or locomotive spouting black smoke. These drawings were then cut and various colored tissue paper pasted inside the box to cover the cut-out figure. A two- or three-inch hole was cut in the lid over a candle which had been cemented to the bottom of the box. A piece of cord was fastened to the front of the box in order that when night came and the candle was lit, the box could be pulled up and down the sidewalk for entertainment of all. Needless to relate, when the first lantern box appeared, the idea spread like fever among all the kids in the neighborhood, and by the following night there were enough lantern boxes on hand to form a long parade.

In looking back, I don't believe I can recall any period in our childhood when one or the other of us was not making something for our use or enjoyment. My brothers and I had each made a model sailboat and other ship models. My brothers sometimes teamed up on a project, such as when they constructed Morse telegraph sets and communicated between their room and the basement. They also made a heliograph by which they could send Morse code signals, and, in this connection, it should be remembered that at that time the heliograph was a standard piece of equipment for the Signal Corps of the U.S. Army.

About this same time, my brother Parker made a small induction coil which was quite successful in producing an electric shock. Parker would gather a group of the neighborhood kids and have them join hands in an open circle. Each kid at the end was given an electrode connected to the induction coil and then the current was turned on. The laughter and shrieking and jumping around as the high frequency current passed through their bodies was a sight to behold. After a minute or two one kid was sure to loosen his grip on his neighbor's hand, thus opening the circuit and stopping the shock sensation. For a moment this would leave members of the group loudly trying to describe to the others just what he had felt, all amid laughter and fun. Then Parker would get them to join hands again and then turn on the switch. The girls began to drop out after the first or second experience, but the boys never seemed to get enough.

Christmas was always a big event in our home, and I shall never understand how my parents survived this annual event. After we kids had been sent to bed on Christmas Eve they had to set up and decorate a fir or spruce tree, bring the presents out of hiding and distribute them and then fill and hang five stockings. The electric tree lights did not come into general use until we were much older; so, after we were all dressed in the morning, Father would go down to the living room and light the small candles attached to the branches of the tree. When all were lit and he opened the living room door we rushed gleefully down the stairs and mother would indicate to us where our presents were piled. After a little while when the candles had burned about halfway down father would extinguish the flames in order that we could light the tree again on New Year's Eve.

One Christmas, when I was about six years old I received an Irish Mail hand car which was propelled by pushing and pulling an upright lever and was steered by the feet resting on a pivoted front axle. This was a fine gift which brought much happiness, as well as exercise to me and my friends. Later, my brother John, who was very clever with tools, extended the length of the frame, added another seat and propulsion lever, thus converting it into a two-passenger vehicle which added to its popularity in the neighborhood.

However, we had other means of transportation, Giggy's father owned a large sheep and goat ranch out near San Angelo. When Gig was about five years old his father instructed his ranch manager to select the finest Angora male goat, have him broken to harness and shipped to Galveston. Eventually the goat, harness and a small sulky arrived and were presented to Gig on his sixth birthday, much to the delight of Gig and his friends. The goat was a large, beautiful creature and was always gentle and well behaved. We all took turns riding in the little sulky, but as this was limited to only one rider at a time this lack of sociability was overcome a year later by the arrival of a small replica of the famous Studebaker farm wagon in which two or three boys could share the thrill of riding all over the neighborhood.

A few years later, however, this was supplanted by a new and better means of transportation. It happened one Christmas morning when a boy named Sawyer who lived two blocks from our house awoke and found no Christmas stocking or other gifts for him under the tree. His parents, of course, acted as mystified as Sawyer and finally suggested that perhaps Santa had stopped to rest out in the old carriage house and absentmindedly might have left his gifts out there. When the door was opened they were greeted by a friendly bray, and there stood a large, sleek donkey hitched to a two-wheeled cart large enough to carry three boys in addition to the driver. There was a Christmas wreath around the donkey's neck and Sawyer's bulging stocking was suspended from one of the shafts of the cart. Immediately the donkey was named Christmas and was soon known and petted by all the kids. Many times we would ride him bareback, frequently carrying two or three boys at a time.

When each of us kids became eight years of age we were considered mature enough to handle a bicycle safely, and the following Christmas my first bicycle, fairly glistening in all its bright paint and nickel plate, was waiting for me under the tree. From this moment until I went off to college, I was never without a bicycle.

It was about this time that the roller skate craze began

to sweep the country and Galveston soon had a splendid rink and I can painfully remember my first effort to remain upright on ball-bearing wheels. While the fad was new my brothers and sisters and I would be allowed to go to the public rink where we and our friends soon gained proficiency and confidence. It was not many weeks after that when we all managed to buy skates of our own, and from then on, a concrete sidewalk or well-paved street was an invitation to get a fast and wild game of hockey under way.

When I was ten years old the first amusement park was constructed. This consisted of a large figure eight roller coaster, a ferris wheel, a merry-go-round and other attractions; but, the one which immediately captured our admiration was a miniature steam railway. This ran on small rails around the circumference of the park, pulling three or four open coaches in which the passengers rode. This was all that was needed to inspire my brothers and me to convert our backyard into an amusement park. With a large supply of old lumber which the wood sawyer had not attacked, it was not long before we had constructed a bicycle shoot-the-chute and a railroad that started from an elevated platform at the top of the high board fence, ran down an inclined track, across the yard and about thirty feet into the basement.

The first consisted of a runway of curved flour barrel staves, from the roof of the chicken house down an incline with two dips in it to the middle of the yard. We had to walk our bicycles up but the ride down at top speed enabled one to coast clear across the yard after coming to ground level. The railroad consisted of a small flat car with flanged wheels which ran on a wooden track which my brothers laboriously ripped out of some one-inch-thick boards by hand. With a kid seated on the car at the top of the platform, a push would start him racing down the incline with momentum enough to coast to the end of the line in the basement. Like most activities in our yard this started out as a commercial venture, with a charge of one cent a ride, but it was not long before all the spare change of the neighborhood kids had been spent and the project was left for all to enjoy without charge.

Another venture which also had a short life developed from the ever-present appetite of a growing boy — the restaurant business. We had a large wall tent in which we were allowed to sleep out at night and to cook our own meals, camp style. We soon learned to fry potatoes, hot cakes, bacon and eggs, and occasionally a fish or two. One day, my brothers, who were considered large enough to go down to the bay by themselves, ran into an unusual streak of luck, and came home with about a bushel of small croakers and piggies which were considered too small by Mother to prepare for her table. So, we cleaned and scaled the fish and packed them in salt and posted a sign on the front of our tent: HANNA'S RESTAURANT — ROUND MEALS 1¢ — SQUARE MEALS 2¢. A small table was set up in one end of the tent and a stove at the other, and for several days the kids of the neighborhood gorged themselves on fried fish and potatoes. The lack of variety in the menu, however, caused operations to cease before there were any damage suits for food poisoning, and we put the tent back into use for our private campout.

On rainy days when our backyard would be empty of any playmates, I would spend much time reading. Stevenson's *Kidnapped* and *Treasure Island* had special appeal to me, and I must have read the latter five or six times. *Robinson Crusoe* and *Swiss Family Robinson* were also favorites of mine as were *Ivanhoe*, Mark Twain's *Tom Sawyer* and *Life on the Mississippi* which I must have read several times during that period.

56

After the splendid Rosenberg Library was completed I was a constant borrower. Here I found books on camping and woodcraft by Beard and Ernest Thompson Seton, and scores of others. During the winter months the library scheduled a series of lectures, usually illustrated by stereopticon slides projected from the balcony to a screen on the lecture platform. The subjects of these lectures varied widely, but I don't believe I ever missed one of them.

When I was twelve years old I became eligible to join the boys' physical training class at the Y.M.C.A. The class was conducted by a full-time physical instructor having the title of professor but we kids shortened it to "Fess" whenever addressing him. The gymnasium was well supplied with the best equipment available and classes were held three times a week, and for two hours we enjoyed the combination of exercise with indoor sports of various kinds. We had calisthenics, tumbling, Indian clubs, dumbbells, weight, parallel and horizontal bars, basketball, handball and many other games, always winding up the class with a shower and a swim in the pool. Over the gym floor there was an oval balcony around which was an indoor track. Here we were taught the fundamentals of sprinting and relay racing. Other track sports were held on the gym floor, such as broad jump, high jump, pole vaulting and shot put. Since there were no organized sports in the public schools at this time, these classes at the Y contributed much.

About the time I joined the Y, the Boy Scouts organization had just come into existence and I became a member of the first troop in Galveston. It was an activity that appealed strongly to me but there was the problem of obtaining and keeping good leadership, there being no paid officials or financial support from the community, and as might be expected we failed to derive much from this activity.

Looking back to those days, it seems that there was never a time that my oldest brother John was not building a boat of some kind. His first was a small kyak. Then he built a canvas-covered canoe. This was followed by a sixteen-foot, double-ended, St. Lawrence river skiff. For this, he had ordered from a manufacturer in Michigan a set of full-size patterns and the necessary lumber and hardware, and he started work in our basement. It was of lapstrake construction, which meant that each plank overlapped the plank below it and had to be fastened to it as well as to the ribs. Copper nails about one inch long were used to fasten the planks to each other, and the end of each nail had to be clinched as it came through. To accomplish this, I would get inside the frame of the boat and hold a heavy flatiron opposite the point where the nail penetrated; the nail struck the flatiron, bent and clinched itself.

Getting back to the canvas canoe, however, it had just been completed and the paint hardly dry when a tremendous cloudburst arrived one afternoon which flooded the streets from curb to curb. The downpour stopped as suddenly as it had started, and summoning several of the other kids we carried the canoe down the alley to Fourteenth Street and launched it into the flood. It floated like a swan until the water had drained off. We were nearly swamped a number of times by more eager passengers than the canoe could carry. When we finally had to drag the canoe out of the ditch onto the sidewalk we noticed that the ground was sprinkled with thousands of silvery minnows of some particular species. These had unquestionably come down with the rain which, it later developed, was the result of a waterspout out in the gulf. As the base of the funnel swept across the surface it sucked up the fish along with tons of water which fell as rain when the disturbance passed over land.

58

When Becky decided to share a house with some members of her family, Father had the old servant's house torn down and constructed a new building in order that we could keep our horse and buggy at home. For many years they had been kept at the livery stable downtown where the horse was well cared for, the harness kept oiled and its brass buckles polished and the buggy washed and polished as often as necessary. Each morning, promptly at eight o'clock, a Negro boy would drive the horse and buggy to our house and secure it to a hitching post at the curb. Then going around to the back of the buggy he would unfasten a bicycle with specially made iron towing arms and return to the livery stable to make another delivery. At whatever time of the day or night that Father had no further use for the vehicle he would telephone the livery stable and in a few minutes the boy would appear, fasten his bicycle to the rear of the buggy and drive off.

After the construction of our new carriage house and stable, it became my job to get up early and hitch up old Maud and drive around to the front of the house and tie her to the hitching post. I didn't object to this as it added substantially to my allowance. Father taught me how to curry, comb and brush her sleek coat and how much oats and hay to feed her. Before starting back to the office after dinner Father would often take her an apple or a lump of sugar, and, in the summer, whenever we had watermelon Maud would always receive a big chunk which she would guzzle delightedly, letting the excess juice and saliva dribble out of the corners of her mouth down to her lips. Whenever Father would not need the buggy in the afternoon I would unhitch it, put a riding bridle on Maud and ride her bareback all over the neighborhood, sometimes with one or two of my friends seated behind me.

As might be expected, however, this was just too good

59

to last. Father had decided to buy a car, and old Maud was sold to Grandma. Her stall and manger were ripped out and the stable converted to a garage. The change for me was not too hard to take, for at that age and era, an automobile was far more thrilling than anything else; nor did I lose my job, for instead of having to get up and feed and polish old Maud I had to polish the brass headlights, windshield braces and dust off the body of the car inside and out. Several years later Father taught me to drive and he and I would go miles down the beach for an afternoon of surf fishing.

The day finally came when we were to leave elementary school and go to what is now known as junior high school. This building was across the street from the high school, and because of lack of room we were compelled to take our recess period on the high school campus. As each new class arrived, the first recess was always spent in undergoing what the older boys of the high school called an initiation. The newcomers were gathered in a group and informed that if we wanted to use their campus for the next nine months we would have to run the gauntlet; they would be perfectly fair, they said, and if any of us did not choose to undergo the initiation we were free to leave the campus and never come back. As there was no other place we could have spent our recesses during the next nine months the choice to be made was obvious. The older boys then formed two long lines about four feet apart facing each other and removed their belts. The first newcomer was ushered in at the head of the line and told to run. About six feet behind another member of our class would be pushed into the slot, then another, and so on. We all ran as fast as we could, of course, and when the older boys plied their belts with all the speed and strength they were capable of, my experience indicated that only about half of the blows actually landed on us.

Another school initiation that I recall occurred whenever a boy donned his first pair of long pants. Unlike the blue jeans of today which a boy may wear at any age, the customary dress for young boys was knickers or plus fours with a coat, sweater or jacket. When he finally reached that gawky age when his longer legs made him begin to take on the appearance of a scarecrow he might change to long pants overnight. When two of my close friends had made the change and I spoke to Mother about it and stated I thought it was about time I made the change also, she said, "Well, I think that would be nice, Jim, but before we reach any definite decision on the matter I think that this is something you should discuss with your father." Well, I had learned several years earlier that whenever I had any special request to make I always got a more sympathetic hearing if I went to his office and discussed the matter than I would get if I presented my problem after he came home; so, away I went. He listened understandingly to my story and indicated his full agreement. After I thanked him I went as fast as my bicycle could carry me to the store where we bought our clothes. I selected a nice suit and some extra pants, charged them to Father's account, and then waited impatiently until they were delivered the next afternoon. The following day I appeared at school in long pants at last, but not without some trepidation, for I knew what lay ahead at recess — my initiation! When recess came the older boys pounced on me as a cat on a mouse and threw me down on the grass. One or two boys would each grasp an arm and leg while I was lying on my back, and at the count of three they would jerk me up as high as possible and then let me drop, just breaking the fall about an inch above the ground. All this was repeated again, and on the third and last flight upward they were not careful in breaking the fall and my body hit the grass with quite a thump. I got up joining them in their laughter and brushing the leaves from my new clothes. As they clapped me on the shoulders I felt wonderful.

Chapter 6

How We Spent Our Sundays

Religion in our family when I was a kid was regarded rather seriously as it was with most Presbyterians of that era. We were required to go to Sunday school from the time we were little more than infants until the time came for us to go off to college. Just before we reached our teens we were expected to attend church also. There were many things taught us that I never understood until long after I had reached manhood, and some that I do not yet comprehend. Many of the hymns which we had to learn and which we sang at many Sunday school sessions contained words which had absolutely no meaning to me as a child, but I loved music and enjoyed the singing of them. Looking back, it is easy to see that many of the volunteer teachers knew nothing of the proper method of teaching nor of the learning process of little children, but who, no doubt, derived much inner satisfaction from the belief that they were truly carrying out the Lord's command to spread the Gospel. For example, can a six- or seven-year-old child understand what the poet meant when he said, "Rock of Ages cleft for me, let me hide myself in Thee"? During my childhood, I must have sung that line at Sunday school and church hundreds of times, but during all that time I never understood or was told what the line meant. True I could always picture a big rock but the word *cleft* simply did not exist in the child's vocabulary, or, for that matter, in the day-to-day vocabulary of the average adult. And so I just sang, too timid to ask my teacher the meaning.

The preachers at our church when I was a kid were all of the John Knox variety, and I sat through many a sermon in a state of fear and wonder, and later, in doubt. Many a sermon was pitched on the theme of giving one's hand to God before it was too late; and to this day I have an unshakable fear of being too late, whether it be to catch an aeroplane or attend a business conference. Once a year there was always a series of revival services, the spring roundup of all mavericks, and these exhortations were filled with warnings of hellfire, brimstone and eternal damnation if one did not respond before it was too late. The fears thus aroused hardly left us kids with any choice whatever if one wished to avoid such a terrible fate.

Sunday for us was a day of quiet reverence. When we came home from church we always had a big Sunday dinner, the climax of which was usually ice cream. This had to be ordered the day before from the ice cream factory and was delivered just before dinner in a large cylindrical container submerged in a wooden tub of crushed ice and salt. At dessert time, the cook would bring the large loaf to the table on a platter, and father would slice it like bread, placing a thick circular slab on a plate and pass it around the table until we had all been served.

After dinner, however, the rest of the day had to be spent quietly: no yelling, shouting or noisy play, nor could we do anything which would be disrespectful of the Sabbath. This meant that we usually had to spend the rest of the day in reading, drawing or painting with our water colors; we were not allowed to go to the homes of our friends, and their visits to our house were discouraged by the limits placed on our own activities.

For the older boys, ten to sixteen, the Y.M.C.A. conducted religious meetings every Sunday afternoon known as the B.G.M. — Boys' Gospel Meetings. These were conducted by the general secretary of the Y, who was an ordained minister but without a church. For two or three years I and two or three of my friends attended these meetings, largely, perhaps, because they were the only accepted form of diversion permitted outside the home. We would sing one or two of the more popular hymns, and then old white-haired Dr. Palmer would deliver a fifteen- or twenty-minute sermon on the old theme of repent before it is too late. Another hymn, followed by a prayer for our redemption, would end the meeting. I shall never forget, however, that in one of his sermons, he related how on two occasions he had seen and talked with God. As I recall now, it was shortly after this revelation that I dropped out of the B.G.M.

At the time we were little children Mother taught us the "Now I lay me down to sleep" prayer, and from then on until we were quite big kids, the last thing we did at night was to kneel down by the side of our beds and repeat that prayer. Then lovingly, Mother would tuck us in and kiss us good night.

For Mother, religion was a very precious thing, a subject upon which she rarely spoke; but when she did, it was always with the utmost reverence. While we were required to attend Sunday school and church neither parent ever tried to force their religious belief on us, doubtlessly feeling that having exposed us to all that was available, the matter was fundamentally one that each person must make up his own mind for himself as he grew into maturity.

In father's early years he had been a staunch member of the church and had been elected a deacon, but when a disagreement arose regarding some business affairs of the church, his attendance at services gradually shrank to zero. Mother and Father had been the first couple to be married in the new church after it was completed, and I am sure that his refusal to participate in the affairs of the church hurt her very much. But in all my life I never heard her utter a word of criticism. Indeed, the only reference to the matter was made by my Aunt Tuncie, a Baptist like her father, who had come to spend the day with us one Monday. She and Mother were seated out on the south gallery where a cool breeze was blowing as they chatted and darned our stockings. After a brief lull in the conversation Mother said with a note of happiness in her voice, "Oh, did you hear that John took me to church yesterday?" Without glancing up from her sewing, Aunt Tuncie said, "Humph! It's a wonder the whole roof didn't fall in!"

Chapter 7

Life at Grandma's

Grandma lived about seven blocks from our house and I have very happy memories of my many visits there during my early childhood. The house was generally referred to within the family as "Grandma's" because it was constructed to the rigid specifications of her father, my Great-Grandfather Davie, and given to her by him. It was a large house of solid brick construction with the outside walls stuccoed or plastered with cement. At ground level there was a full length basement divided into a number of rooms, one of which was the kitchen, located directly under the dining room on the first floor where all of the meals were received on a dumbwaiter from below.

To enter the house, the tall basement made it necessary to climb a flight of ten or twelve steps to a small tiled porch, then through the double storm doors, into a small vestibule where one encountered the double inner doors, each having a tall panel of red Florentine glass. Here, one entered a small reception area with stairs leading up to the second floor, and on the left, a parlor separated from the living room by tall sliding doors. The end of the hall opened onto a wide L-shaped gallery, and, to the right, into a room which, today, we would call a den. From here one entered the large dining room.

On the second floor there were three large bedrooms equipped with a marble top lavatory in one corner, and each having a door opening onto the wide L-shaped upper gallery in order that each room could have access to the bathroom containing a tub and lavatory, which opened only onto the gallery and to a separate toilet room down at the end of the porch.

Grandma and Grandpa, of course, occupied the largest or master bedroom. Across the hall, the bedroom over the den was occupied by their divorced daughter Agnes, or Aunt Tuncie as we all called her, and her daughter Dorothy, who was about the same age as my older sister Margaret. The adjoining room was the solitary domain of a sad-faced, wrinkled old lady whom we all referred to as Auntie Flood. Actually, she was a cousin of Grandma's somewhere along the line and had had a tragic marriage experience, though I did not learn of this until many years later. The north end of the hall opened into a large trunk room, about ten by sixteen feet. Since the arrival of Auntie Flood, the trunks had been shifted around and this had been made into the bedroom of my Uncle Sam who was at that time attending The University of Texas Medical College.

Down in the basement, in addition to the kitchen, one

of the rooms was occupied by the old Negro cook, Venus Lee.

The head of the household was, of course, Grandma. She was fairly large (she seemed so to us children at the time) and was still quite attractive. As she quietly went about supervising the daily household chores she always wore an apron over her dress which could readily be slipped off if company should drop in, and she always carried with her a large key ring to which there were attached at least twenty or thirty keys. There was always an air of self-confidence about her, like the true matriarch she was; and while she could be firm when occasion demanded, she could also be tender and compassionate.

Grandpa, who had been a captain of artillery in the army of Northern Virginia and was later captured and imprisoned by the Yankees, reminded me of the pictures I had seen of his commander, General Lee. His white beard and the gentleness that always showed from his eyes and face were like Lee's, and he still practiced all the virtues of Southern chivalry, always deferring to Grandma's wishes. For example, he never smoked inside the house as, to do so, might be offensive to the ladies, and, regardless of the weather, always went out on the gallery where he kept his pipe and tobacco, and here he stayed until he had finished his smoke. Every Sunday afternoon he would come to our house to visit for an hour or two with Mother. This was an event we children always looked forward to, for he never left the house without presenting to each of us a nickel. He was always kind and gentle with everyone, and if he ever felt any bitterness over the war years he did not give voice to it; nor did we ever ask him to relate any of his war experiences, for to do so might bring up unhappy memories.

There was one member of the household who could

never, never forget nor forgive, although, as she had not been born until the year 1873, she could not possibly have suffered any of the war's privations. Yet Aunt Tuncie was an unreconstructed rebel if there was ever one, no doubt still carrying childhood memories of the horrifying tales of the Reconstruction Era told by the old ladies. On one of the occasions when our family had been invited to Grandma's for dinner, and during the usual dinner table conversations, someone happened to mention that February 12 would be Lincoln's birthday. At this remark, Aunt Tuncie glared around the table and said emphatically, "I should prefer that that name never be mentioned in this house again. He has brought enough misery to the South without our having to be reminded of it." No one said anything, but even to my tender years, I was only eight years old at the time, I seemed to sense a breakdown in communication somewhere; for in our dinner table conversations at my home, I had gathered that President Lincoln was really a fine man and that the injustices and persecutions of the Reconstruction Era would never have occurred had Lincoln not been killed. But that was Aunt Tuncie. She was a Baptist, hard-shelled, that is, and the family had long since learned that it was useless to try to discuss either religion or politics with her. She was always right. She was right when she married Uncle Fred, and she was equally right when, after her daughter Dorothy was born, she divorced him. After I was somewhat older my father told me that Uncle Fred was really a very fine man, and that his only fault was his unwillingness to let Aunt Tuncie remake him according to her own pattern. She came back to live at Grandma's, firm in the belief forever after that all men except her father were beasts.

Dorothy and my sister Margaret, about the time they started to school, would spend alternate Saturdays together, first at Grandma's and then at our house. Sometimes I would go along, the three of us painting with water colors, trying to write poems or reading *St. Nicholas* magazines, of which Grandma must have had about twenty bound volumes. Dorothy was always kind and thoughtful, and I always enjoyed these visits very much. Unlike the rest of us, however, Dorothy was sent to Miss Jackie Andrew's Private School, and it was not until she finished the elementary grades that she got a taste of public school atmosphere. She had a talent for art and later spent two years at the Chicago Art Institute, her mother accompanying her the whole time.

We saw very little of my Uncle Sam during this period of my life, as he was kept well occupied attending lectures, laboratories and dissecting cadavers at the medical college where he was rated a brilliant student. Many of the students lived in our neighborhood, and about sundown every evening we would see them in groups of three or four going back to their rooms, some carrying a femur, a skull or a complete vertebra strung on a cord. Not infrequently a small gang of tough kids would follow about half a block behind yelling, "Yeah, bone jugglers, bone jugglers!" If a group of students stopped and turned as if to pursue their tormentors the gang would flee precipitously with wild yells.

If I happened to be out in our front yard early in the morning I would frequently see Uncle Sam on his way to classes, and always got a cheery greeting. One morning just after my eighth birthday when I had received a cast iron toy cannon, Uncle Sam passed by and I proudly showed it to him. He looked it over carefully and then told me that if I would be there the following morning he would bring some gunpowder and we would fire it. I was there, bright and early, and when he came he reached into his coat pocket and brought out a twelve-gauge shotgun shell. He uncrimped the end and poured eight or ten buckshot into my hand; then, removing the wadding, he poured a small quantity of the gunpowder into the muzzle of my little cannon and primed the firing hole, after stuffing some of the wadding in the muzzle to contain the powder. We placed the cannon on the ground and Uncle Sam put a lighted match to the touchhole. The result was a loud "bang," with much smoke and the little cannon recoiling about ten or twelve inches. I believe I was too thrilled to even thank him, and Uncle Sam went on to his classes at the university.

The last member of Grandma's establishment whom I should describe briefly was Venus Lee, the cook. She had high cheekbones and a beak nose so common to the American Indian, but was very dark skinned. She had been purchased as a slave by my great-grandfather, but after the war she refused to leave him and after his death she attached herself to Grandma and stayed with her until her death, sometime in the 1920s. She lived in one of the rooms in the basement which opened onto a hall which led to the kitchen, the latter a place which none except Grandma might enter without her permission.

Venus could neither read nor write, but if there were ever any gourmet delight she could not cook I never knew what it was. If there were something new that Grandma wanted she had only to describe it in general terms, mention some of the principal ingredients, and Venus could produce it to perfection.

And how people did eat in those days! It was a custom of long standing for my family to have dinner at Grandma's on Thanksgiving Day, and Grandma's family would come to our house for Christmas dinner. Of course, there were other days during the year when we exchanged visits, but the amount and variety of food consumed differed little from those prime holidays. Grandma's Thanksgiving Day dinner consisted in part of a huge turkey, a baked ham, potatoes, rice and four or five fresh vegetables, mince, apple and lemon meringue pies, three different kinds of cake, fresh fruits of all kinds and a plum pudding or ice cream. At our house on Christmas, it was pretty much the same, beginning with oyster soup, rich with minced bacon, parsley, onions and celery followed by a waldorf salad, and then turkey and a baked ham with enough cloves stuck into its surface to make it resemble a shorn hedgehog. Sometimes, in place of the baked ham, Father managed to get a suckling pig which was roasted with a red apple between its jaws, a small carrot sticking out of each ear and a red cherry placed in each eye socket. It was difficult to carve one of these for the meat was so tender it practically fell away from the bones. There were the usual vegetables, pickles, olives and chowchow. Then followed several kinds of desserts of chocolate pecan cake and mince and apple pies. But our mince pie was always different from that which we had at Grandma's, for at some time during the morning Father always managed to have a private conference with Pearl, our cook, at which time he handed her a cup of one hundred proof bourbon with instructions to put it in the mincemeat just before the pie was ready to put in the oven. On every occasion, when we had gotten down to eating pie, Aunt Tuncie always asked, "Sister, where do you get your mincemeat? This certainly has a delightful flavor!" Good Baptist that she was, I doubt seriously if she would have ever taken another bite had she known of Father's instructions to Pearl.

Aunt Tuncie's aversion to President Lincoln and her bitterness about the late war is not hard to understand if we remember that many of the old aristocratic families of

Galveston had actually suffered not only from the war itself but from the shameful atrocities that occurred during the period of Reconstruction. To keep alive the memories of our Southern men and their gallant deeds, an organization known as the United Daughters of the Confederacy had been organized throughout the South, and at this period of my life, my great-Aunt Aggie, who lived only one block down the street from Grandma's, was head of the local chapter. One of their primary objectives at this period was to organize a children's auxiliary of the Daughters which was to be known as "The Immortal Six Hundred" Chapter, after a memorable, but probably tragic military engagement of Confederate troops. I, and my sister Margaret, Dorothy and all of the other children of the prominent Southern families of Galveston were drafted into this organization, and for several years had to attend monthly meetings where we were compelled to listen to accounts of the brave deeds of our ancestors, and wind up the meetings singing "Dixie."

Chapter 8

My Visits to the Ranch

I believe there are relatively few city-bred kids who ever have the opportunity to visit a ranch, and so I count myself very fortunate to have spent two summer vacations on my brother Parker's ranch in the Texas panhandle, twelve miles west of the little town of Canyon.

The first of these visits occurred when I was about thirteen years old and Parker was still in the process of getting things organized and in production. The land he had bought had only two buildings, a barn with adjacent corral and a dugout house consisting of several rooms where we lived. This was a square frame house sunk about four feet into the earth to protect it from the severe blizzards of winter and the strong winds of the high plains which came sweeping down from Montana and the Dakotas to the plains of Texas each winter.

Cooking was done on an oil stove, but when winter came a small cast iron heating stove, for which the only fuel available was buffalo chips or dried cow droppings which we gathered from the pasture, kept the dugout snug and warm.

Besides a couple of milk cows there were only a few head of cattle at this time as our first concern was to plant and cultivate several hundred acres with maize and kafir corn to carry a herd of cattle through the bitter winter when there was no grass and as extra food for the work horses which had to pull the plow, the cultivator and the big farm wagon.

When my brother had bought the ranch he invited an old college chum from Texas Agricultural and Mechanical College to come visit him while getting started, and while I was there the three of us shared whatever work there was to be done. In addition to cultivating the grain field, there were barbed wire fences to be built or repaired, doctoring the navals or other maladies of young calves, occasionally repairing the windmill or replacing the sucker rods in the well. There were weekly trips into town for supplies, sometimes in the Model T Ford, and sometimes in the big Studebaker farm wagon.

It was not all work for me. There were times when there was nothing for me to do and I would go for long rides on Parker's fine saddle horse. After he had given me careful instructions in the proper handling of a gun I would take the .22 caliber repeating rifle and wander off into the canyon and shoot at water snakes sunning themselves on the rocks in the creek, or occasionally bring home a rabbit or two. We could hear the coyotes howling at night but rarely saw them in the day time. Once when I was walking along a fence line I was startled by the unmistakable sound of a rattlesnake, and found him only a few feet away coiled up in the shade of one of the cedar fence posts. Taking careful aim with the rifle I blew his head off with one shot and then cut off his rattles to keep for a trophy.

Two years later I was to spend another summer at the ranch. In the meantime my brother had married his old sweetheart and he had brought her out to the ranch where in spite of many pioneer hardships, they lived in blissful happiness. Soon after her arrival they selected plans for their new home and old Judge Turner, who lived in a small town on the other side of the canyon, was given the contract to build the home where they were to spend many years together. Although I must have added much to her household duties, Lydia always gave me the love and tenderness of an older sister, and many times went far out of the way to make my stay a happy one.

By this time Parker had gotten things well organized and other than keeping the row crops well cultivated there was not too much work required. Roy, the friend who had visited Parker when he first bought the ranch, had since left to establish a ranch of his own in South Texas, but he was replaced by another old A&M friend who came out and spent several months. Jack was a very friendly chap, and together we did a lot of clowning and general mischief. One day he got the idea that we should have a tennis court and so, with Parker running the scraper to clear the sod, we soon had a hard, smooth court on the west side of the house. With the net in place and the standard court markings made with white lime, we had the job completed. For the rest of the summer, after all the chores were done, we had wild games.

The only modern convenience the ranch lacked was a

telephone. The office in Canyon told us that we had two options: either build a line the twelve miles to the city limits where they would connect with it, or get permission from the owners of some existing farmer-owned lines running out a few miles in our general direction and connect on to it. The nearest line to the ranch was seven or eight miles away, but as this was the lesser of the two evils we obtained permission to connect. Then we purchased the necessary wire, insulators and magneto telephone and loading all these items together with necessary tools, nails and other materials into the big farm wagon, we set out early the next morning to construct the line. No poles were necessary as we planned to follow the local practice of nailing an insulator to the fence posts and attaching the line wire to these, the other side of the circuit being grounded at both ends. All went well until about ten o'clock when I began to feel thirsty and rummaged in the wagon for the water jug; it was not there. So I went back to work trying to keep my mind from thinking any more about my growing thirst. As we progressed from fence post to fence post my thirst for water increased and I could not help but recall all the places I had ever enjoyed fresh water. My brother suggested I lie down in the shade under the wagon, which I did; but this did not help. I could remember the water in the swimming hole in the creek and the tons and tons of cool water in the pool at the Y.M.C.A. back home, and these memories only served to torture me the more. Sometime about noon as I got up to allow the wagon to advance I happened to glance to the south and saw a beautiful blue lake in the distance and started running toward it, shouting to the others and pointing. Parker caught up with and stopped me, stating that it was only a mirage, a phenomenon we were to observe from time to time during the rest of the summer. He assured me that we would not do any more work now but would drive to the nearest ranch house which was not far away. When we finally arrived, it was the freshest, sweetest and most delightful water I had ever drunk. While cautioning me not to drink too much, Parker was splashing the cool water on my head and the back of my neck. Shortly thereafter, we were all seated in the shade eating the lunch Lydia had packed under the seat in the wagon. Eventually the line was completed, the telephone installed and the company assigned a code ring of two long and one short as our number.

When I came to the ranch I brought with me a set of plans for constructing a biplane glider which I eventually completed. I had visions of leaping off the rim of the canyon and soaring through the air like the eagles and hawks we frequently saw in motionless flight. The day finally came when it was finished just as Lydia rang the bell calling us to lunch. So I left it lying on the ground over by the dugout and ran to the house to answer the call to lunch. While I was helping to clean up the dishes Parker had gone over to the feedlot to let the horse into the water tank but soon returned with the startling news that my glider had taken off by itself and flew beautifully. He then explained that a little twister or "dust devil" had come along, picked up my glider and sent it aloft for several hundred feet. The "dust devil" then collapsed as suddenly as it had started, leaving my glider to sail gracefully down to the ground where it smashed into a tangled mass of splinters, cloth and wires, never to fly again. It was heartbreaking for me at the time but I have often thought since then that that little twister was sent by the gods instead of the devil to save me from making a fatal leap off the canyon rim.

While hunting down in the canyon one day I noticed

some raccoon tracks in the mud by the bank of the creek. I had always wanted a raccoon for a pet, but even if I had seen the animal I could not have captured it without a trap. Recalling having seen a small steel trap hanging up in the barn, I brought it back to the creek, fastened the three-foot chain securely, set the jaws of the trap and covered it with tall grass and reeds. Two days passed before I had an opportunity to go back to the trap and when I did I saw that a circle of trodden-down grass and reeds limited by the length of the chain had been beaten flat, but there was no coon. As I drew closer I could see that the trap had been sprung, and from the outside of the jaws there protruding a furry and splintered stump of bone, while on the inside of the jaws protruded unharmed the left hand of the coon. Thus, to escape the trap it had been forced to gnaw the bone of its arm just above the wrist. Needless to say, I have never tried to trap another animal in all my life.

Chapter 9

Social Life When I Was a Kid

In all that I have recalled so far, little has been said about girls in my life as a kid. There were girls, fine ones of my own social set and to whom I always felt a strong attraction. To begin with, when I enrolled in the low first grade in elementary school, there were in my class the three Ms — Mary, Marie and Margaret, already as devoted to each other as I was to become to my friends Gig and Ghent. They were all very pretty and attractive girls with sparkling personalities, and it was only natural that between us three boys and those three girls a bond of friendship was soon established that was to last throughout our lives.

Occasionally, when the three of us were riding our bicycles we would encounter the three Ms riding theirs, with the result that we would wind up at the home of one of them where we would spend the rest of the afternoon in friendly chatter and discussion of recent events at school or other happenings. The three Ms were always immaculately dressed; their hair was wavy; their eyes seemed to sparkle and there was a rosy glow to their cheeks, especially in winter. At that time fashion decreed that red or scarlet jackets were the stylish garb for girls, and the three Ms were so dressed.

One day as Ghent, Gig and I were riding our bicycles around the neighborhood we stopped before crossing one of the main streets when I happened to glance to my right and there, two blocks away, I saw three red jackets on three bicycles crossing the street. "There they are!" I exclaimed. "Let's go catch up with them." Before we could get started, an old Negro woman standing on the curb back of us said, "Effen you boys wants to stay out of trouble you bes' leave them gals alone, cause they's quality folks." Well! I thought to myself, there it was again, that antebellum status label that I had heard Becky use several years before. Certainly, one could not argue with the old mammy's statement.

When we advanced to junior high school, and later on to high school, other girls joined our group: Hortense, Patience, Elizabeth and others who came from some of the fine old homes in other sections of the city. We all mingled together at school and met occasionally at parties and dances. But of all the girls in our social set, the three Ms filled my mind and my heart with the greatest affection and I am sure that, over the years, I had a bad case of puppy love with each one in turn.

One place where we could generally count on meeting them was the weekly dance at the Garten Verein, a social club to which all our families belonged. This was located on a plot of ground about four blocks in area and landscaped like a park with broad lawns, winding gravel walks,

82

trees, shrubs and flowers. Off towards the back of the grounds was a building referred to as the Club House, equipped with bowling alleys, card and domino tables and a bar. About a hundred yards to the south was a dance pavilion, polygonal in shape with windows which could be opened on all sides. In the middle was a fine polished dance floor, and between it and the windows was a wide space around the entire building filled with chairs where the mothers, nurses and chaperones could sit and chat while keeping a watchful eye on their youngsters out on the dance floor. A supply of programs with printed blank lines for each dance and with a small pencil attached by a silk cord and tassel were available just inside the door. If a boy came alone he would ask the girls which dance he could have and her name would be written on the proper line in his program and his name in hers. If the girl had been brought by an escort, then it was his responsibility to see that all lines in her program were filled before the orchestra began to play. If his date was the popular type or especially attractive this was fairly easy to do; but, if she were not, he might find himself having to fill in most of the blank lines on her program with his own name. In either event, when the orchestra began to play, he would take her from her group of admirers or rescue her from the mammas and chaperones and lead her out onto the dance floor. The dance floor held no attraction for the younger boys. Those who had not yet advanced to the long pants stage, would congregate out in the park area where they would compete on the horizontal bar and the swings, or play the whole evening a wild game we called "Hunter and Hare."

Another means of entertainment during this period of my life was a trolley car ride at night. The street railway company had a special car which was used for nothing else; it was decorated from front to rear and from top to bottom with colored lights. It was an open type car with seats which ran across from side to side. It would easily seat eighty to a hundred kids, and after they were loaded, long bars would be lowered to prevent anyone from falling out. As it was open on all sides there was always a summer breeze blowing over the partygoers as the car traversed the tracks through the city. Neither my family nor anyone in our set, that I know of, ever chartered this car for a party, but many nights we could see it in all its brilliant colors speeding past our house.

We did get to go on several hayrides, however, and we enjoyed these very much. A large flat-bottomed truck pulled by a team of stout horses would be chartered for the purpose with the bed or floor filled with fresh, sweet-smelling hay covered to a depth of a foot or more. We kids would pile aboard, seek out chums we wished to sit with and off we would go singing all the songs we knew. Sometimes there would be two big cans of ice cream packed in tubs of ice stowed near the driver, and when we finally came to the beach we would jump down and play tag until the hostess had dished out that ice cream we had all been waiting for. Then back up into the hay to finish the ride home in the moonlight.

About the time my brothers entered high school, a yacht club was organized and our family became members. A club house was constructed on an island across the channel from the wharves and piers. The club purchased a number of small boats for the use of the members, among which were several single and double racing skulls. Just before sundown members would begin to show up at the club, some of the single swains with a date and a box of bonbons under his arm. One of the club's smaller rowboats would be put in the water, the girl would be helped

84

gallantly into the stern, he would take his seat amidships facing his date and would start rowing into the twilight.

There were, of course, many other forms of entertainment: swimming parties, beach parties, birthday parties, Halloween parties and picnics. The railroad company maintained a large picnic area in a grove of giant oaks about twenty miles from Galveston and every year or so our Sunday school would have a picnic there. Our family and Grandma's would join forces for this event, and, as always, there was much food to share with others. The picnic grounds were well supplied with tables and benches, a large pavilion, and swings for little and big kids. Getting all the numberless baskets of food aboard the train, to say nothing of the hundreds of children of all ages, was no mean task. I am convinced that miracles do take place, particularly at picnics held in the name of the church. Belching smoke the engine finally pulled the train out of the station, down through the switchyards to the bay where for two miles we rode above the water on a narrow trestle. Reaching the mainland the engineer opened the throttle, and away we went. As a kid these train rides were the most thrilling and enjoyable part of the whole outing.

With my sad experience with piano lessons one might never think it possible but I could always carry a tune having once heard it. Perhaps I inherited this from my father who loved music all his life. He was a member of the Galveston Quartet Society, a group of about forty or fifty businessmen under competent leadership. Each year they would present a series of public concerts, singing with such precision and harmony that they never failed to fill the auditorium, even though these concerts were full dress affairs. As far back as I can remember I never failed to attend these concerts with Mother and my sisters. To me, this was entertainment at its best. Sometimes the Quartet

Society would vary its concert schedule by presenting a light opera, and I still recall the pride I had in Father when he acted the part of Dick Deadeye in *H.M.S. Pinafore*.

At that time there were a number of communities in Texas which were predominantly German, and each of these towns had its "singing society" or choral club of male voices. At a certain time each year they would all band together, meet in a certain city and hold what was called a Saengerfest, at which there might be as many as several hundred voices singing together. Several times when I was a kid these concerts were held in Galveston and we all attended.

One of the social activities we enjoyed most were the times when there would be guests for dinner. Should any of our friends be present when dinner was announced, Mother always permitted us to invite them to eat with us. This we enjoyed because the conversation at the table seemed to have a new freshness.

We also enjoyed those times when Father brought home one of his friends for dinner, usually on very short notice to Mother. This would have irritated some women, and, on one of her weekly visits, I once heard Aunt Tuncie remark that she would not permit such a practice, to which Mother replied that this was as much Father's home as her own and that she would always do whatever she could to make his guests feel welcome. Some of these guests would inject a bit of humor or a joke or two which brought laughter from all of us; others would relate some interesting experience which we had not heard of before.

One day Father called before starting home and told Mother that she had better set an extra place at the table as he was bringing Judge Turner home for dinner. Mother gave a cheery assent and went about making the necessary arrangements. Suddenly she stopped in her tracks

86

and said to herself, "Judge Turner? I don't know anyone by that name. I wonder who he could be." But she had entirely forgotten having met this man two years before when she and Father were visiting my brother Parker on his ranch out in West Texas. By occupation Turner was a carpenter and, indeed, had constructed the new home where Parker welcomed his bride. The title of Judge was conferred by virtue of the fact that he had been elected and re-elected for many terms as justice of the peace for his precinct in the county. He lived just about four miles from Parker's ranch on the other side of the Tierra Blanca Canyon at the bottom of which a small creek irrigated the cottonwood trees and the wild grapevines which flourished through the canyon.

At this time there was a strong movement for prohibiting the manufacture and sale of alcoholic drinks, and while the Eighteenth Amendment had not yet been passed, Texas had a local option law and was dry territory from the western half of Texas to the New Mexico border. But there in the canyon were all those deep purple grapes, and year after year Turner had gathered them and converted them into delicious and potent wine. While he did not regard this as a commercial venture he did occasionally sell a gallon jug or a small oaken keg to a close friend, and the word eventually leaked back to members of the temperance group who complained to the sheriff of this open violation of the law and demanded that Turner be arrested and punished. Under such pressure the sheriff conducted many raids on Judge Turner's place but could never find any evidence. Turner had many friends around the courthouse back at the county seat who promptly called him whenever a raid was scheduled, thus permitting the removal of all evidence to a safe hiding place before the sheriff or his deputies arrived.

On one occasion, however, the warning call failed to reach him. He was caught red handed, arrested, tried and sentenced to a year in the state penitentiary at Huntsville. During this period of incarceration his term of justice of the peace expired; but his faithful friends rallied to his aid and succeeded in re-electing him for another term. A few months later he was released on good behavior and it was at this time that he decided to call on the parents of his good neighbor Parker before returning home to resume his official duties. It was then that Father brought him home to dinner. When Mother went to the front door to welcome the pair her face turned red as she recognized the man she had met several years before out at the ranch and her usual personal warmth became somewhat chilled. While not rabid on the subject she was mildly in favor of the temperance movement and she had never showed much sympathy for lawbreakers. By the time Father came home from work in the evening she was still a little wrought up over the affair and I heard her exclaim, "John, how in the world could you do such a thing! The idea of you bringing a known law breaker, a criminal, an ex-convict into our home! To eat at our table! And just think of it, to allow a man just out of the penitentiary to associate with our children. I have never been so shocked in all my life!"

I could see that Father was not too disturbed over his act of kindness to Judge Turner but only over the fact that he had unintentionally hurt Mother. He knew that over the years Turner had eaten many meals in Parker's home and he in Turner's home, and that it would have been an unpardonable breach of hospitality had he not invited Turner to our home. He tried to explain this to Mother but he could see that she was not wholly convinced. "He had no right to break the law and make that wine in the first place," said Mother.

"Well, as to that," Father replied softly, "that seems to raise the question as to which law we are to observe, man's or God's. You know that the Good Book says, 'Thou shalt drink a little wine for thy stomach's sake and thy frequent infirmities.' " Nothing more was said, but we kids long remembered the thrill of having eaten dinner with a real ex-convict.

Prior to the beginning of World War I some of the battleships of our navy would visit Galveston, and whenever this occurred my parents were always invited to the formal parties given aboard ship by the officers. The day before the party was scheduled, a handsome young ensign, immaculate in his white duck uniform, would appear at our front door to deliver a written invitation from the captain, addressed to my parents. The next night I would act as chauffeur and drive them down to Pier 22 where, with other guests, they would be assisted aboard the captain's barge and taken out to the battleship. I never saw them when they returned home for it was usually very late, but at breakfast the next morning Mother would describe what a nice party it was, how the ship's band provided music all evening, how gallant the officers were and which of their old friends they had enjoyed meeting there.

On one of these occasions our cook, who was also responsible for sweeping and dusting the downstairs part of the house, failed to show up, so Mother took over these duties. It was a hot, summer morning and by ten o'clock the perspiration was streaming down her face and her house dress and apron had become a bit dishevelled. Just then, the front doorbell rang and, as there was none of us available at the moment, Mother went to answer the ring. As she approached the open door she could see through the screen the cool white uniform of a naval officer. She realized that he too, had seen her and, as she described the incident to us at the dinner table, she said that she wanted to drop through the floor or run away, but she couldn't; as she reached the door she said very politely, "Yes?"

The young officer bowed and asked, "Mrs. Hanna?"

"Oh, no," answered Mother, "This is Bridget, sir."

The officer held out an envelope and said, with a slight smile on his lips, "Captain Graves of the *Texas* sends his compliments. Will you please give this to Mrs. Hanna?"

We all roared with laughter but complimented Mother on her quick thinking. After her report on the party the following day we asked her if the young officer had remembered her and asked, "May I have the pleasure of the next dance, Bridget?"

Chapter 10

Our Days on the Water

Living so near salt water there can be little wonder that we spent so much of our lives watching the various activities on the wharves or swimming in the gulf or sailing on the bay. All of the activities of shipping, the noises, the odors, perhaps influenced by the books we read, accounted for this. Then, too, my great-grandfather had crossed the Atlantic in 1827 in a sailing vessel, and my grandfather and my great-uncle had been captains of river steamboats on the Ohio and Mississippi rivers.

Whatever the cause I was always attracted to any maritime activities going on in the port and constantly felt the call of the water. For example, when I was old enough to go down to the wharves alone I spent many hours there watching the ships from all over the world loading or discharging their cargoes.

Some were rusty, old tramp steamers eager to pick up a cargo wherever it could be found. Others were ships of British, German or American lines with regularly scheduled sailings, such as the fine freighters of the Morgan Line which was owned by the Southern Pacific Railroad, and those of the Mallory Line, which included some passenger ships. Historically, it is interesting to note here that the Mallory ships were all named after Texas rivers: the *Nueces,* the *San Marcos,* the *San Jacinto,* the *Rio Grande,* for example.

The scenes here on the wharves always filled me with excitement as I watched the Negro longshoremen, stripped to the waist, bodies glistening with sweat, as they pushed their hand trucks from the warehouse to shipside. With cargo booms and tackle swung out over the wharf, cargo nets were lifted from the hold of the ship and dropped swiftly to the apron of the wharf from which it was snatched as soon as filled and then let down into the ship's hold. All this was accompanied by the rattle and screech of block and tackle and the chugging escape of steam as the small engines up on deck turned the winches. Sometimes the cargo nets would be filled with five-hundred-pound bales of cotton or heavy crates of machinery or slabs of red copper. But in all these operations there always seemed to be an atmosphere of hurry, hurry, hurry, as if the ship had to put to sea at once. There were times when this was indeed true and the longshoremen and stevedores worked far into the night.

To me, the most exciting times on the wharf were the days when a North German Lloyds steamer would come into port bringing several hundred steerage passengers. These were the people from Poland, Germany, Russia and

92

the Czechoslovakian provinces who had come to make a new home for themselves in the central and western part of Texas under the liberal immigration laws then in effect.

After the ship had been tied up to the wharf there would be a long delay while immigration authorities checked the papers of all the passengers. A motley crowd of men, women and children then descended onto the apron of the wharf, all carrying their possessions tied up in blankets, sacks and wicker baskets. Some wore the colorful native costumes of their homeland but most appeared very poor. The men were usually unshaven and some wore heavy beards. Here on the wharf they milled around or huddled in family groups guarding their bags and bundles, waiting with enquiring eyes.

There were always a number of Jews and Rabbi Cohen could always be seen weaving through the crowd seeking those who could speak only Yiddish and who needed the rabbi's reassuring help in directing them on their way. There were also the representatives of the big land companies seeking those whom they had helped and in many cases arranged for their transportation. On the edge of the crowd there were a few better dressed people who had arrived on some previous voyage, hopefully searching with their eyes for some relative. These meetings were always tearful yet happy, restoring confidence to the new arrivals.

Eventually everyone was set on the proper course to his final destination and the longshoremen took their place on the wharf apron to begin unloading such cargo as the German ship had brought. At home that night I could not dispel the scene I had witnessed that day and wondered at the courage it must have taken to enable most of these people to come to a new country where they could neither speak nor understand its strange language. It was much later before I learned that, for these people, no new

93

country could possibly hold for them the miseries and injustices they had experienced in the lands they had left.

There was a much different scene, however, down at Pier 22 where the red snapper fleet docked. These were graceful two-masted schooners similar in design to the much famed Gloucester fishing boats which sailed to the Grand Banks of Newfoundland in search of cod, and like them, the snapper boats could stay out at sea for weeks at a time. Before leaving port their holds would be almost filled with large blocks of ice to preserve the fish until their return to port. Sailing far out into the gulf they would search for the snapper banks, high submarine plateaus or ridges on the continental shelf, where the beautiful pinkish-red fish would congregate by the thousands. When they returned to port with holds full of fish well iced down, I would frequently go down to Pier 22 and watch while the catch was unloaded, packed with ice into barrels and loaded onto freight trains for shipment to many cities throughout the country.

Of course, there were days when I longed to sign on with one of the great steamers, or even with a snapper schooner, but there was wise counsel at home and I had to content myself with smaller vessels.

My brother John had a small sloop which he kept anchored off the club, and many an evening he would show up at the supper table with a fresh, pink coat of sunburn. Later John bought a twenty-foot sloop from the captain of one of the Mallory Line ships, and on weekends and during the summer vacations we would take long, overnight cruises on the bay. John had built an open cuddy over the forward half of the cockpit which afforded some shelter in the event a shower came up; but when he went to the university in the fall it was my job to go over to the club and bail out any accumulation of water, which I

94

would have gladly done for nothing but he insisted on paying me a dollar a month.

For several years I had owned a small twelve-foot sloop I had built myself and kept in a corner of the slip at Pier 16. I could sail this out into the protected channel, up and down the wharves, being careful to avoid some hustling tugboat or a passing steamer. This was all very well, but I wanted something larger so I could cruise in the upper bay which sometimes got very rough. Finally convincing John of my problem he designed an eighteen-foot sloop with a trunk cabin over the forward half of the cockpit. I succeeded in building this in our backyard and got it launched in time to sail her fifty miles up the bay to the Y.M.C.A.'s summer camp at LaPorte. With a strong south wind we made it to the camp, not, however, without nearly becoming shipwrecked when we ran onto an oyster reef about midway in our trip and damaged the rudder. My companion and I got the boat clear of the reef but had to sail the remaining distance under jib alone, using an oar to steer.

On another occasion my friend Taylor and I had been fishing out in the bay and on the way home decided to stop at Pelican Island and cook our supper. The sun had not yet approached the horizon; so we knew we would have plenty of time to get home before dark. We beached the boat at the edge of the water, threw the anchor up in the grass and started to prepare our supper of bacon, fish, bread and beans. When we had finished and gone back to the sloop we found that the tide had gone out and left us high and dry. The sun was just dropping below the horizon and it would be dark in a few minutes. We strained and tugged at the boat but could not budge her. Hours passed, and with each passing minute I realized the worry my parents were going through. We were perfectly safe where we were and I knew it; but my parents did not. They had long since finished their supper and were now probably gathered in the living room discussing the sad fate of our drowning. When I envisioned this sort of thing I thought it would be best if I never did get home, for I was sure that Father would half kill me for causing them so much worry. There was still nothing we could do but wait for the turn of the tide, and I was not too anxious to see this happen. About 9:30 we noticed a huge boat approaching the island, pointing a searchlight along the shore. It soon picked up our boat with the water just beginning to lap against the stern. As we approached the boat we immediately recognized it as the Coast Guard Patrol. In no time at all we were afloat again and being towed to our mooring in the slip at the foot of Tenth Street. When we finally got home I was sure that all hell was going to break loose the minute I opened the front door. But it didn't — Mother just put her arms around us and asked if we were hungry, and Father just stood there smiling at us. When we had apologetically explained what had happened, Father said that he hadn't been worried; it was a perfectly calm night, and that unless we had been run down by a steamer, something hardly likely to happen, he felt we were perfectly safe, but, just to be sure, he had phoned the Coast Guard and asked them to look around for us. Well, I thought . . . but never mind.

These adventures with my boat were to end soon, however, for the weather bureau announced in August that another strong hurricane was approaching the Texas coast. Later bulletins stated that it would pass inland at or near Galveston; so I went down to the Tenth Street slip and made the boat as secure as possible. Even then the wind was blowing with increasing intensity out of the northeast, and during the night it struck with all its fury. When morning came and the flood waters had subsided I went down to the bay to see how my boat had fared, but it, along with all the others, had completely vanished. Some distance back from the shore there was a large pile of wreckage, broken boards, pieces of masts and spars and damaged rigging. I searched carefully through this pile of wreckage but found not a single splinter that I could identify as part of my little sloop. The big seawall had proved itself, having saved the city from the tremendous loss of life and property like that which occurred in 1900. The loss of my boat was heartbreaking, but I soon realized that I had only one more year at home before going off to college and did not attempt to replace my loss.

Chapter 11

I Leave Home and Grow Up

The day finally came when we were to graduate from high school, and it was time for me to decide on what sort of a career I wanted to follow and to get ready for college in the fall. English had always been a fairly easy course for me, probably because I had spent so much of my life reading good books and because I had never experienced any trouble in writing and, indeed, liked to do it. I, therefore, decided that I should major in journalism. True, I liked the sciences, physics and chemistry, but for some reason, I had great difficulty in visualizing mathematics, and that seemed to rule out the possibility of taking any branch of engineering. Indeed, I came very near not graduating with my friends, when I flunked my trigonometry final — but after an almost tearful plea to my math teacher he willingly gave me a second "final," which I passed, and I received my diploma with the rest of the kids in my class.

I had a good friend next door who was a junior at the William Marsh Rice Institute for the Advancement of Science, Letters and Art — now changed several years ago to Rice University, at Houston. That early name of the school was certainly impressive to a kid dreaming of his future, and Tom convinced me that Rice had one of the highest scholastic ratings. I sent in my application for entrance in the fall session of 1916 and was accepted.

With Tom's help, therefore, I began to make lists of things I would need and to complete plans for leaving home. Sadly, I realized that this meant leaving my old friends, but this could not be helped when we were all growing up and soon would no longer be kids. Good old Gig had gone to A&M the year before, Ghent was signing up for The University of Texas where he wanted to play football while majoring in pre-med, and my friend Margaret, too, had decided to go to The University of Texas. Leon and two others from my class were going to enroll at Rice, but they were not members of our little group; so it would not be like having one of the old tried and true friends to pal around with. This, I realized, was one of the most disheartening things about growing up, and as I thought about it, I began to realize that part of this business of growing up was the necessity of making new acquaintances and friends for as long as we may live into the future.

The fifty-mile trip to Houston was made on the electric interurban, a mode of transportation which had developed in many cities through the country during the first decade of the century, but which, even now, was feeling the effects of competition from increasing use of the automobile and good highways. In a few years this competition would cause

99

abandonment of the interurban service; however this did not happen until long after I had left Rice and I found it very convenient in going back home occasionally for a weekend visit and for the various holidays.

Registration was simple and I was assigned to a nice room on the third floor of one of the dormitories. The majority of students there were juniors and seniors who, after Tom's introduction, gave me a very friendly welcome. The chap who was to share my room was a big disappointment to me but, fortunately, after about a week of classes, he dropped out and returned to his home. My assignment to a table in the commons enabled me to meet five additional students; so it was not long before I had the feeling of belonging. Meals were served in the commons three times a day and there was always plenty of good food.

The courses I had selected were, with one exception, well taught and very interesting. The course in medieval history, unfortunately, was taught very much as it had been back in grade school, a test in one's ability to memorize dates and places with no emphasis on historical events and of their effect on civilization. French was difficult for me but I felt that a knowledge of the language and its literature was essential to one who expected to make writing his career; so I struggled on with it. Chemistry and biology courses had capable instructors and the laboratories were well equipped and supplied. My course in English stressed composition and I acquired much that was helpful. Several of my themes or compositions were selected by the instructor for reading to the class, although I recall some embarrassment when he criticized my use of the word *stink*, suggesting that a better choice would have been *stench*. About every week or two we would have a very interesting lecture by Dr. Axon who was at that time the world's greatest authority on William Shakespeare.

100

Christmas came and I spent a delightful week at home. My brothers were back for the holidays from A&M and Texas, and my sister Margaret from Mary Baldwin, and I gained the impression that they now regarded me as having risen to equal status with them, which added to the general congeniality of the group. There were several parties during the week and my reunion with my old friends was a most happy one. Somehow, the feeling grew in me that during the three months I had been away from home I had really begun to grow up and would soon no longer be considered just a kid.

It is doubtful, however, if anyone who was familiar with some of the youthful, not to say diabolic, tricks we younger men cooked up from time to time would have agreed that there had been any increase in maturity whatever. For example, the cold winter night when we waited up on the third floor of our dormitory stairwell with a large paper sack full of water for the night watchman to come in to punch his clock on the ground floor directly below us. Of course, he never knew whether the bomb was released from the second or third floor, and by the time he arrived at our end of the hall everyone was soundly asleep, or feigning it.

The stunt that gave us the biggest thrill of all, I always felt, was the night we put soap on the car tracks opposite Rice's main gate. To get back to school after a date in Houston one rode the regular trolleys out to Eagle Street, the end of the developed area of Houston, and transferred to a shuttle which ran out to Bellaire, about five miles away, with the stop at Rice's main gate about midway between. Immediately after taking on his passengers at Eagle Street the motorman invariably threw his controller wide open and let the old car go rattling and wobbling at full speed until within a hundred feet or so of Rice's main gate. He would then pull the controller around to zero, applying the compressed air to his brakes and come to a sudden screeching halt to let the students off. This was always a trying experience, one we thought should be eliminated as a public service. So, we mixed up two buckets of thick, gooey soap and we brushed it on the rails from a point where the air was usually applied to the breaks, on past the Rice stop and about four or five blocks beyond. We hid behind the broad gate pillars on each side just in time to see the trolley's headlight approaching in the distance. As usual the motorman cut his power and shot the compressed air to the brakes at the usual point, but nothing happened. With its brakes locked, the car failed to slow down and went coasting speedily past the Rice stop and on down the tracks for nearly a quarter of a mile. For a few minutes we were convulsed with laughter; our plan had worked, and as we imagined the look of surprise and chagrin on that motorman's face, we became convulsed with laughter again and simply rolled around on the ground. Suddenly, however, we heard approaching voices, and fearing that the students, some of whom were bound to be upperclassmen, might not have enjoyed that quarter mile walk back to the gate, we muffled our laughter and retreated to the dorm before anyone caught sight of us.

After our return from the Christmas holidays the bull sessions in the dormitories became quieter and took on a more serious tone. The war in Europe, which had now been going on for three years, appeared much more serious for the Allied Forces, and many of the upperclassmen expressed the opinion that if Germany did not relax her belligerent attitude towards the United States we would be in the conflict before the end of the year. That estimate proved optimistic, however, for, with the torpedoing of our shipping, climaxed by the sinking of the *Lusitania*,

102

war was declared in April. The bull sessions really took on a more gloomy atmosphere now, for we knew that sooner or later we would all be expected to help defend our country, and none of us was happy about the thought of having our education interrupted in this manner. Many of the seniors, architects, engineers and chemists, had already formulated plans for going into business after graduation in June, and they knew without anyone having to tell them that all these plans would have to be abandoned. Some felt that they might be old men by the time the war would be over, and they would have to go back to school and take refresher courses not withstanding the degrees which would be awarded them in just a few months. A few had weddings planned for June, and now they did not know if or when they would ever take place. And so it went.

No draft of men had yet been authorized, only a call for volunteers. At that time there was no such thing as a government R.O.T.C. course in the universities, but the secretary of war issued a statement that all colleges and universities wishing to organize military training units would be furnished rifles and uniforms, although no one could be spared from the army to serve as instructor. My neighbor Tom and another chap from Galveston had each had several years at military prep schools; both had good leadership qualities and the general respect of the student body. After a meeting had been called and the government's offer explained, enough men signed up for the training to make two companies of infantry. The clothing, hats and rifles arrived shortly thereafter, and we were soon learning to drill and master the manual of arms. By the end of school the two companies were quite proficient.

By that time the army had developed the Officer Training Camps program offering a second lieutenant's commission upon successful completion of the course to those willing to volunteer for the duration. Many of my friends at Rice entered these training camps, but I had always felt that my sailing experience, my love of ships and the sea, best qualified me for the navy, and I began to inquire around.

In midsummer news came to me that the navy had followed the army's pattern and had established officer training schools for volunteers of suitable background experience who would be given a commission as ensign upon successful completion of the course. This was just what I had been looking for, and so, on September 17, 1917, I was sworn in, just eighteen days after my twentieth birthday.

Well, what happened after that is another story. Obviously what lay ahead for me could hardly be regarded as a part of my childhood, and to continue on with a full account of my life would defeat my purpose of trying to picture for you just what it was like when I was a kid.

The Author

James Scott Hanna, Sr.
1897-1972

James Scott Hanna, son of John Hanna and Frances Virginia Griffin Hanna, was born August 30, 1897, in Galveston, Texas, where he lived for much of the early part of his life. He attended Rice University in Houston, Texas during the period of World War I, but interrupted his education to enlist in the Navy and fight that "war to end all wars." When he returned from sea duty in the Cruiser and Transport Force as a naval officer, he worked for two years in the citrus industry in Florida, where he met and married Elfreda Brandon.

He joined the Southwestern Bell Telephone Company in Galveston in June of 1921 and this was to become a lifetime career. He served lengthy periods in the Galveston,

Houston, and Dallas offices in various executive positions. As Commercial Engineer for the State of Texas, he was responsible for growth and development forecasts on which all engineering and construction in the Texas operating area were based. During this time he testified before the Federal Communications Commission in Washington concerning engineering details of the first ship-to-shore telephone.

In the early 1950s, when the telephone company became deeply involved in the communications network of utmost importance to the security of the United States, Mr. Hanna was quite active in the SAGE Intercontinental Defense System and worked on this project in the Dallas area for a number of years. It is with no small pride that the children of James Hanna, Sr. look back on his lengthy career with Southwestern Bell and realize that he made a lifetime contribution to this miracle.

Just prior to his retirement from Southwestern Bell Telephone Company, Mr. Hanna became Vice-President of Southwestern Engineering and Equipment Company, a position which he held until his death in December of 1972. This was, in many respects, a second and subsidiary career to his work with Bell, for his contributions to this organization, both managerial and technical, were substantial.

At a time when many men were breaking out their fishing rods, Mr. Hanna was not only involved in this new career but was busily engaged in a number of far ranging hobbies as well as the authorship of several books on genealogy and the history of the Southwest. Hobbies which he pursued at various times — some of them continuously until the date of his death — included archaeology of Mexico and the Mid East, photography, collection of antiquities, art, good books, classical music, sculpturing and the creation of ceramic pieces which he fired in his own furnace.

After he retired, James Hanna moved to Lake Travis, not far from the small town of Leander, where he constructed a very attractive home which commanded a striking view of the lake and the distant terrain of the Texas Hill Country, so beautiful in all seasons of the year.

He was now able to launch into a study of genealogy in depth, particularly as it applied to a direct history, going back many hundreds of years to England. He traveled extensively in the United States and Great Britain gathering data for a genealogy of his wife's family, *The Brandon Family of Southwest Florida.* This book was published in 1969. He also published a genealogy of the Hanna family, *The Descendants of James and Mary Cupples Hanna* and, at the time of his death, he was writing a history of his Grandmother Griffin's family. Another book, on which he had done considerable study, was to be on the rock houses of pioneer families in Texas. The architecture of these early dwellings (many of which are still around) fascinated him. He talked about photographing them and writing up a history of each home.

While living at Lake Travis, Mr. Hanna became increasingly interested in the civilization of ancient Mexico. On one occasion he made a several month's trip down into the southern portions of that country, for he was a very serious student of both present day and pre-Columbian Mexican history and of the Aztec and Maya civilizations.

In closing, it should be left with the reader that, above all, James Hanna was a loving husband and father and dearly beloved by all associated with him. He and his wife, Elfreda Brandon Hanna, reared and educated four children: James Scott Hanna, Jr. (married to the former Donna Lee Maples); Marjorie (Mrs. Fred Harmon); Ian

Brandon Hanna (married to the former Emily E. Dillon); Barbara (Mrs. Corydon W. Bell). The fact that all members of the family, both by birth and by marriage, are recognized for their cultural and professional contributions to the community is a good index of the kind of persons the father and mother were and the type of family atmosphere that existed during their lives together.

Fred Harmon

108